MEN *of*
CHARACTER

Paul

Living for the
Call of Christ

GENE A. GETZ

FOREWORD BY JIM MOORE

BROADMAN
&HOLMAN
PUBLISHERS

Nashville, Tennessee

© 2000 by Gene A. Getz
Printed in the United States of America

Ten-digit ISBN: 0805418180
Thirteen-digit ISBN: 9780805418187

Published by Broadman & Holman Publishers, Nashville, Tennessee
Editorial Team: Vicki Crumpton, Janis Whipple, Kim Overcash
Typesetting: Desktop Miracles, Stowe, Vermont

Dewey Decimal Classification: 225.9
Subject Heading: BIBLE STUDY—PAUL / PAUL, THE APOSTLE,
SAINT / BIBLE. NEW TESTAMENT EPISTLES OF PAUL
Library of Congress Card Catalog Number: 99-044909

Unless otherwise stated all Scripture citation is from the NIV, the Holy
Bible, New International Version, copyright © 1973, 1978, 1984 by
International Bible Society. Also cited is NASB, the New American
Standard Bible, © the Lockman Foundation, 1960, 1962, 1963,
1968, 1971, 1972, 1973, 1975, 1977; used by permission.

Library of Congress Cataloging-in-Publication Data
Getz, Gene A.
    Paul : living for the call of Christ / Gene A. Getz.
        p.   cm. — (Men of character : 12)
    Includes bibliographical references.
    ISBN 0-8054-1818-0 (pbk.)
    1. Paul, the Apostle, Saint. 2. Bible. N.T. Epistles of Paul—
Criticism, interpretation, etc. I. Title
    BS2506.G48   2000
    225.9'2—dc21   [B]

                                                      99-044909
                                                           CIP

12 13 14 15   10 09 08 07 06

I am privileged to dedicate this study on the life of the apostle Paul to my good friend Jim Moore, a man who has demonstrated that a Christian can be a businessman of the highest caliber and consistently exemplify Jesus Christ in his attitudes and actions. For a number of years we've worked together planning the highlight of our year—a Bible-study ski trip for men at one of the great recreational areas in the United States, Beaver Creek, Colorado. Our purpose is to have fun on the ski slopes and, more importantly, to spend quality time in the Scriptures each morning and evening, culminating with a wonderful time of sharing and praying in our final evening together. Thanks, Jim, for modeling the principles in this study that flow from the life of one of the greatest Christians who ever lived—the apostle Paul.

Paul

Contents

Foreword

While we can certainly learn valuable life lessons from studying all biblical men and women, the apostle Paul's life and letters strike a chord very close to my own personal walk with Jesus Christ.

First, as with all of us, Paul did not have the advantage of close personal contacts with our Lord during His earthly ministry. Second, I also identify with the extended period of time Paul was driven by his own earthly ambitions. And though my conversion certainly was not as dramatic as Paul's, the Lord also stepped into my life and redirected me when I was heading in the exact opposite direction God wanted me to go. While we have not held the clothes of those who murdered Stephen, we can all look back at the depth of our sinful nature and realize what it was like not to have experienced the redeeming work of the Holy Spirit. But if we have had a personal encounter with the Lord Jesus, then we can say with Paul: "Therefore if any man is in Christ, he is a new creature; the old things passed away; behold, new things have come" (2 Cor. 5:17, NASB).

Paul has also taught me another lesson: that becoming a Christian is not a life that is always "upward and onward." The "desires of the flesh" are not eradicated. All Christians have vivid memories of really desiring to live for Christ only to experience failure in our personal walk with the Lord. It's at such moments that Paul's words near the end of his life have special meaning for the maturing believer. Writing to the Philippians, he said, "Brethren, I do not regard myself as having laid hold of it yet; but one thing I do: forgetting what lies behind and reaching forward to what lies ahead, I press on toward the goal for the prize of the upward call of God in Christ Jesus" (Phil. 3:13–14, NASB).

This study in Paul's life will help you understand the true meaning of the free gift of salvation and will also help you balance this wonderful gift of life with the responsibility that we all have to "press on toward the goal for the prize" that awaits all faithful Christians.

As my good friend, Gene Getz, unfolds Paul's life in the following pages, it's my prayer that this dynamic New Testament Christian's message will strike the same chords in your life as he has in mine.

Jim Moore
Businessman

A Personal Journey

Shortly after I became a Christian, Paul became one of my major biblical heroes. As a newborn child of God, I quickly developed a hunger to study the Scriptures. I couldn't miss Paul's impact on what I was learning about Christian truth. After all, he penned at least thirteen New Testament letters.

"My God Will Meet All Your Needs" (Phil. 4:19)

I'll never forget one of my first encounters with this dynamic Jew-turned-Christian. I was a junior in high school, 16 years old, and I'd secured a copy of Dr. Kenneth Wuest's commentary on Philippians. With my Bible in one hand and Wuest's explanation (which included what he called "golden nuggets" from the Greek New Testament) in the other, I studied this letter word for word and sentence by sentence. I still remember my new insights.

As a young man who was still learning to speak good English, I was struck by the Greek word *koinonia*—a word Paul used to describe the Philippians' generosity in sharing in his life and ministry (Phil. 1:3–4, 10–19). The "good work" God had begun in their lives (1:6) related directly to their sacrificial spirit in supporting Paul financially after he had left them to go on to Thessalonica (4:14–16). Now once again they were caring for his physical needs.

This truth, more than I realized, laid the groundwork in my heart and soul to motivate me to be a generous Christian and to learn more from Paul regarding God's perfect will for my life. I was also reassured that when I put God and others first with my material possessions, God will take care of me. I was a teenager when I learned this lesson, and now as a senior citizen, I can report that God has never let me down. Paul's words are true: "And my God will meet all your needs according to his glorious riches in Christ Jesus" (Phil. 4:19).

"Who Shall Separate Us from the Love of Christ?" (Rom. 8:35)

My next significant memory is of an experience I had two years later. I was eighteen and a student at Moody Bible Institute. I'd been struggling with my view of eternal life. Since I had been reared in a religious environment that mixed faith and works for salvation, even after I had become a Christian, I didn't know for sure that I had eternal life. Consequently, I was often confused about my relationship with God. My spiritual life was like an emotional roller coaster.

And then something happened. Early one morning I was sitting in my dorm room reading Paul's letter to the Romans. Suddenly I was confronted with a very pointed question that almost jumped off the page: "Who shall separate us from the love of Christ?" Paul asked (Rom. 8:35a).

Just as quickly, Paul's answer rang out loud and clear, not only in chapter 8 but throughout the preceding chapters in this dynamic letter. I was overwhelmed. For the first time, I understood what Abraham understood centuries before—that "we have been justified through faith" apart from works (Rom. 5:1). I now understood that Abraham had been made righteous when he had believed God—not because of any human effort. His salvation experience had happened *before* he was circumcised and *long before* God would give the Ten Commandments to Moses on Mount Sinai.

Like a cool, calm breeze from heaven, I realized that I too had been made righteous by faith in Jesus Christ—just as Abraham (Rom. 5:1). He had looked forward to the cross and resurrection, and I looked back. Though I had received eternal life a couple of years before this wonderful morning experience, I now had the assurance of my salvation apart from my emotional moods, human failures, and spiritual doubts. I *knew* I was saved—then and forever. Paul's answer to this question penetrated my heart with new meaning:

> *Who shall separate us from the love of Christ? Shall trouble or hardship or persecution or famine or nakedness or danger or sword? . . . No, in all these things we are more than conquerors through him who loved us. For I am convinced that neither death nor life, neither angels nor demons, neither the present nor the future, nor any powers, neither height nor depth, nor anything else in all creation, will be able to separate us from the love of God that is in Christ Jesus our Lord. (Rom. 8:35, 37–39)*

I've never forgotten that moment of truth. It changed my life.

The Grace of God (Titus 2:11–14)

A couple more years went by before I had my third life-changing experience with the Lord through Paul's New Testament letters. It happened after I had graduated from Moody Bible Institute. I was involved in radio ministry in Billings, Montana. At the same time, I was finishing my college undergraduate work. Someone had given me a book by John Strombeck entitled *Disciplined by Grace,* an exposition of a paragraph in Paul's letter to Titus.[1]

I had boarded the train in Chicago for a sixteen-hour trip across the great northwestern states. I opened Strombeck's book and began to read and reflect on what he had to say about Paul's words to Titus:

For the grace of God that brings salvation has appeared to all men. It teaches us to say "No" to ungodliness and worldly passions, and to live self-controlled, upright and godly lives in this present age, while we wait for the blessed hope—the glorious appearing of our great God and Savior, Jesus Christ, who gave himself for us to redeem us from all wickedness and to purify for himself a people that are his very own, eager to do what is good. (Titus 2:11–14)

This was another dynamic moment for me with Paul the teacher. Even though I now knew I had eternal life, I still struggled emotionally over the warnings I had heard against this dangerous doctrine. After all, if we are confident we're truly saved—now and eternally—doesn't this mean we can live any way we want? Paul's answer to this question was a definite "No." He also made this point crystal-clear in his letter to the Romans where he raised this very question—and answered it emphatically: "Shall we go on sinning so that grace may increase? By no means! We died to sin; how can we live in it any longer?" (Rom. 6:1b–2).

Paul elaborated on this answer in his letter to Titus. His words penetrated my heart and soul. Another spiritual light went on. How can Christians who truly understand God's mercy in saving them take advantage of God's grace and live an ungodly lifestyle? Somewhere between Chicago, Illinois, and Billings, Montana, I began to comprehend my freedom in Christ. At the same time, I was deeply challenged never to use this marvelous freedom to "indulge" my "sinful nature" (Gal. 5:13). On the contrary, this new spiritual insight motivated me to respond to God's grace with love and holiness.

This life-changing encounter with the Holy Spirit through Paul's words to Titus also eliminated my lingering confusion regarding what it really means to be saved by grace through faith and not by works (Eph. 2:8–9). I also understood more fully his reassuring words to the Ephesians—that once we're saved, "we are God's workmanship, created in Christ Jesus to do good works, which God prepared in advance for us to do" (Eph. 2:10).

"Follow My Example" (1 Cor. 11:1)

Researching the life of Paul, teaching these lessons to my own people whom I serve at Fellowship Bible Church North, and then writing this book on his life, has, of course, been my most significant and comprehensive encounter with this great apostle and, more importantly, the Lord Jesus Christ. The lessons that flow from Paul's life and ministry are intensely convicting, motivating, and very practical. I now understand more fully his exhortation to the Corinthians and why he could say, "Follow my example, as I follow the example of Christ" (1 Cor. 11:1).

As you read and study this book, hopefully the dynamic "principles to live by" that grow out of a study of Paul's life will impact your life too. If you'll allow God's Spirit to help you apply them in all of your relationships, I'm convinced you'll never be the same again. Furthermore, as you reflect on Paul's life, I challenge you to keep the words he wrote to the Philippians in the forefront of your mind, words that reflect his own goals as a Christian:

> *Not that I have already obtained all this, or have already been made perfect, but I press on to take hold of that for which Christ Jesus took hold of me. Brothers, I do not consider myself yet to have taken hold of it. But one thing I do: Forgetting what is behind and straining toward what is ahead, I press on toward the goal to win the prize for which God has called me heavenward in Christ Jesus. (Phil. 3:12–14)*

Table 1
Chronology of Paul's Life

Scripture	Event	Approx. Dates*	Approx. Years*	Paul's Accumulated Age
Acts 22:3a	Birth and Early Years in Tarsus	A.D. 1–13	13	13
Acts 22:3b	Studies in Jerusalem under Gamaliel	A.D. 14–19	6	19
Biblical Logic and Inference	Return to Tarsus as a Tentmaker and Rabbi	A.D. 20–33	13	32
Acts 8:1; 9:1–19	Persecution of Christians and Conversion	A.D. 33–34	1	33
Gal. 1:13–17	Stay in Arabia	A.D. 34–36	3	36
Acts 9:19–22; Gal. 1:17	Return to Damascus	A.D. 37	several months	37
Acts 9:26; Gal. 1:18	Return to Jerusalem	A.D. 38	several months	38
Acts 9:30	Return to Tarsus	A.D. 38–44	6	44
Acts 11:25–26	Joins Barnabas in Antioch	A.D. 45	1	45
Acts 13:1–14:28	First Missionary Journey	A.D. 46–48	3	48
Acts 15:1–35	Council of Jerusalem	A.D. 49	several months	49
Acts 15:36–18:22	Second Missionary Journey	A.D. 49–52	3	52
Acts 18:23–21:16	Third Missionary Journey	A.D. 53–58	6	58
Acts 21:17–23:30	Arrest in Jerusalem	A.D. 58	several months	58
Acts 23:31–26:32	Confinement in Caesarea	A.D. 58–60	2	60
Acts 27:1–28:16	Trip to Rome	A.D. 60–61	1	61
Acts 28:17–31	First Imprisonment in Rome	A.D. 61–63	2	63
Pastoral Epistles	Continued Ministry	A.D. 63–66	3	66
	Martyrdom	A.D. 67	several months	67

*The above dates and Paul's accumulated age are approximate and may vary by several years. However, to simplify remembering these statistics, the years are arranged to coincide with the first year following Christ's birth, and even though Christ was probably born several years before A.D. 1, I've used our current calendar. Therefore, this chart only provides a general frame of reference.

Chapter 1

Sincerely Wrong

I've never met anyone whose sincerity prior to conversion has outdistanced Paul's. But neither have I met anyone who was so woefully mistaken and misguided. Many people who make bad decisions and choices have wrong motives. They know they're wrong. Not so with Paul. He "acted in ignorance and unbelief" (1 Tim. 1:13). With all his heart, he thought he was right—which is one of the greatest lessons all of us can learn from Paul's life. It's possible to be very earnest and fervent in our beliefs and behavior—but dead wrong!

In a very small way, I can identify with Paul. I was born and reared in a religious community where I was taught that only people who participated in the life of this community would ever have a chance of going to heaven. Most everyone I knew who shared this experience had the same belief system. In fact, if you doubted this theological viewpoint and made it public, you would be subject to severe criticism and even alienation. And, if you continued down this "wayward path," you would eventually be subject to various forms of church discipline—including excommunication.

As I grew up within this very tightly-knit and closed culture, I initially believed wholeheartedly what I'd been taught; and when I turned sixteen, I became an official member of this religious sect. I was as sincere as anyone could be—but over time, I came to the rather startling conclusion that I was sincerely wrong.

My search for truth led me to study at Moody Bible Institute in Chicago. It was there I experienced in a very powerful way the true meaning of what Jesus taught—that "the truth will set you free" (John 8:32). Though I was already a Christian, in many respects my studies at Moody constituted my Damascus Road experience. I met Jesus Christ in a new way as I studied Paul's life. He too was headed down a wrong religious path. Everything changed when he met the Lord personally, but not until after he had committed some horrible crimes against the church.

A Conspiracy Against Stephen (Acts 6:8–14)

Paul first walked on stage in the biblical record in the midst of a very intense and hostile scene. Stephen, one of the seven men who had been selected and appointed to care for the Grecian widows in the dynamic and growing church in Jerusalem (Acts 6:1–7), had just been dragged bodily to the outskirts of the city (7:57–58).

It was a gruesome scene. Various members of the Jewish Sanhedrin—a body of seventy-one key leaders in Israel—picked up stones and pelted Stephen until he died. Ironically, they believed they were doing the will of God.

While they were carrying out this horrible atrocity, they "laid their clothes at the feet of a young man named Saul," which was Paul's Jewish name (7:58). He had just approved of Stephen's death (8:1). This means that the high priest in Israel and other members of the Sanhedrin had given him authority to oversee this vicious attack. Consequently, Paul carried out this awful task as if he'd been given direct orders from God Himself. He was merciless.

False Witnesses

Sometime after Stephen had been assigned to distribute food to the neglected widows, he began to carry out a very intentional evangelistic ministry. He utilized his unique spiritual gifts to perform "great wonders and miraculous signs among the people" (6:8; see also Heb. 2:3–4). However, he faced serious opposition, particularly from some of the Grecian Jews. They were members of the "Synagogue of the Freedmen" (6:9), a group impossible to identify precisely, except that some of them were from the province of Cilicia. Since Paul grew up in this area of the Roman Empire, it's feasible that some of these men attended the same synagogue in Tarsus where Paul may have served as a rabbi after he studied under Gamaliel.

Regardless of the circumstances surrounding their potential relationship with Paul, these men deeply resented what Stephen was preaching and teaching. They went toe-to-toe with him and argued against his Messianic message. However, in spite of their efforts to silence this deacon-turned-preacher, "they could not stand up against his wisdom or the Spirit by whom he spoke" (6:10).

As with so many people who cannot explain away arguments that substantiate the story of Christianity, pride and anger enveloped their souls. Rather than admitting their inability to invalidate Stephen's message regarding Jesus Christ, and since they could not give a satisfactory explanation regarding the powerful miracles that verified this message, they resorted to the same behavior demonstrated by their fellow Jews against the Lord Himself. On the sly, they found people who would become false witnesses (Matt. 26:59–60; Mark 14:55–59). More specifically, "they secretly persuaded some men to say, 'We have heard Stephen speak words of blasphemy against Moses and against God'" (6:11).

Sadly, this deceptive strategy paid off. Resentment and hatred towards Stephen spread through Jerusalem, and eventually a number of religious leaders "seized" him "and brought him before the Sanhedrin" (6:12). Again false witnesses spoke out against Stephen, distorting his message (6:13–14).

What happened next must have been awesome—even chilling. Everyone—including Saul of Tarsus—could see that something strange was happening. Stephen's face glowed with a supernatural presence, which no doubt explains why the high priest gave him opportunity to defend himself (6:15–7:1). Moved by the Holy Spirit, Stephen succinctly and clearly outlined Israel's story (7:2–50), which set the stage for his blistering exhortation that accused these men and their ilk of rejecting God's prophetic messengers for centuries. "You always resist the Holy Spirit!" he proclaimed. "Was there ever a prophet your fathers did not persecute?" (7:51–52). And when he accused them of murdering the true Messiah, Stephen's audience suddenly went ballistic. And just as suddenly—at least in the biblical record—Saul (Paul) boldly stepped forward as the delegated representative to organize and lead the brutal attack on Stephen which resulted in his death (7:57–8:1).

An Old Testament Precedent (Lev. 24:10–16)

This traumatic scene was a first-century replay of an Old Testament event. Centuries before, a young man whose mother was an Israelite and whose father was an Egyptian attacked another young man whose parents were both Israelites. The first son had already rejected the God who had brought them out of Egypt. He blasphemed God's name, which probably means he actually cursed the Lord.

Since God was in the process of revealing His civil laws to Israel, this rebellious young man was taken into custody until God specifically and directly rendered His will regarding this kind of sacrilegious attitude. The Lord then spoke to Moses directly, indicating that whether a person was "alien or native-born," when a person "blasphemes the Name, he must be put to death" (Lev. 24:16). God made it frighteningly clear He would not tolerate this kind of behavior among His people.

Stephen was accused of this same kind of blasphemy before the Sanhedrin. Every one of these seventy-one men would have been aware of this Old Testament event recorded in Leviticus. They represented the religious intelligentsia in Israel. And as a well-educated Jew, Paul had probably memorized this section of the law.

Tragically, the accusations had been maliciously fabricated. Motivated by false information, calloused hearts, and their own spiritual blindness, the members of this Jewish court proceeded to participate in taking Stephen's life. Though many of them may have actually known the truth about Stephen and that they were acting inappropriately, Paul at least truly believed he was doing God a service. As he later testified, he "acted in ignorance" (1 Tim. 1:13).

A Great Persecution (Acts 8:1–3)

Paul was relentless in his efforts to stomp out this growing Christian movement. He not only approved of Stephen's death, but he launched an all-out war against his fellow Jews who had put their faith in Jesus Christ. He "began to destroy the church" by "going from house to house," and literally dragged "both men and women" through the streets of Jerusalem and locked them up in prison (Acts 8:3). Years later, after Paul had become a Christian, he testified publicly in Jerusalem that he had "put many of the saints in prison, and when they were put to death" he cast his "vote against them" just as he had done with Stephen (Acts 26:10). He even went a step further and "tried to force them to blaspheme" in order to have a valid reason—according to the law—to sentence them to death. When he resorted to this kind of manipulation, Paul's belief that he was right led him to rationalize and to do what so many people do when they desperately want to achieve their goal. In their minds, the end justifies the means.

The persecution that Paul launched was so intense that the majority of Christians had to flee for their lives, leaving Jerusalem in order to discover a place of refuge in other parts of Judea and even in Samaria (8:1). However, the greater the persecution, the more Christianity grew and survived. Luke has recorded that "those who had been scattered preached the word wherever they went" (8:4).

A Young Man Named Saul (Acts 7:58)

As stated earlier, Paul's involvement in Stephen's martyr-dom is the first reference to him in the biblical record. But how and why did he suddenly walk on stage in Jerusalem assuming this powerful role? When did he come to the Holy City? Had he ever met Jesus Christ personally or at least heard Him teach? Though we can't answer all of these questions definitively, we have enough details from Paul's own letters, as well as from Luke's record in the Book of Acts, to be able to reconstruct much of his life before this event—a reconstruction which in turn helps us understand what the driving force was behind his actions. Secular and Jewish history also corroborate some of what we know from the biblical documents.

Birthplace and Dual Citizenship

We don't know exactly how old Paul was when he stood on the outskirts of Jerusalem and approved of Stephen's death. However, most Bible students believe he was between thirty and thirty-five years of age (see chronology chart on p. 6). This would mean he was born approximately the same time as Jesus Christ but in a totally different area of the Roman Empire. A number of years after he became a Christian and a great missionary to the Gentile world, he returned to Jerusalem and addressed a large crowd of people and stated, "I am a Jew, from Tarsus in Cilicia, a citizen of no ordinary city" (Acts 21:39).

When Paul stated that Tarsus was "no ordinary city," he was referring to an historical fact. Serving as the capital of Cilicia, this great metroplex numbered approximately 500,000 people when Paul lived there (see fig. 1).

The Taurus Mountains were located approximately twenty-five miles north, yielding rich minerals and timber. In addition, Tarsus was noted for its leather goods and a cloth identified as cilicium, which came from the hair of black goats.

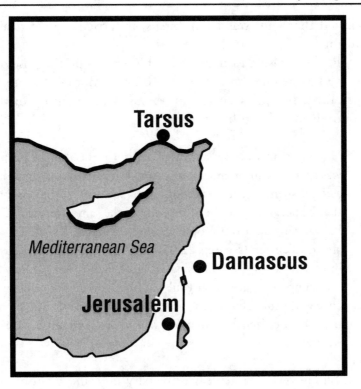

Figure 1
Tarsus—Paul's Birthplace

This cloth was used to make tents—a trade Paul evidently learned as a young apprentice to his father. In fact, after he became a missionary and ran short of money gifts to continue his ministry full-time, he at times kept body and soul together as a tentmaker (Acts 18:1–5).

Tarsus had been self-governing from the time it was a Greek city-state, and when the Romans conquered Greece, they honored Tarsus and gave the city the standing of *Libera Civitas,* Latin words that mean a "free city." At the time Paul was born, this standing gave the people of Tarsus the right to continue to govern themselves and to be free from many Roman taxes. Consequently, when Paul eventually did missionary work throughout the Roman Empire, and when government leaders learned that Paul was from Tarsus, it carried a great deal of weight.

Paul was also a Roman citizen by birth, a privilege held by only a few people throughout the Empire. But even more significantly, he was a citizen of Tarsus. Commenting on this honor, Robert Picirilli writes:

> A person who is a citizen of a city [in the Roman Empire] was therefore automatically a person of influence. . . . Inasmuch as Paul spent . . . his boyhood in Tarsus, we can be confident that he became a citizen of that city in the same way that he got his citizenship from Rome, namely, because his father was already a citizen (see Acts 22:25–29). This has some very strong implications for our understanding of Paul's background. For one thing, it suggests that Paul was from a family of some influence and probably wealth. One thing required for inclusion in the role of citizens was that one had to own property of certain worth.[1]

Tarsus was also a great university city, more prominent than Athens and Alexandria. Its people pursued culture avidly, and many studied philosophy and the liberal arts. At some point in time, Paul was exposed to this educational environment which, as we'll see in this study, was reflected in his sermons and correspondence.

Family Background

Paul was definitely the product of two cultures. Not only was he reared in the Greco-Roman environment, but he was also strictly Jewish. In the same address Paul delivered in Jerusalem after his missionary journeys, he stated, "I am a Jew, born in Tarsus of Cilicia" (22:3).

Paul's father was an Orthodox Jew, a fact which had more impact on him than the environment in general. He grew up learning to speak and write *koine* Greek, the common language of the Roman Empire. However, he was also exposed to

Hebrew from the time he was born. This is why he identified himself as "a Hebrew of Hebrews" (Phil. 3:5). Even though he was a Grecian Jew—a term used to describe Israelites who lived in other parts of the Roman world outside of Jerusalem and Judea—he had command of the Hebrew tongue. In actuality, this language is identified as Aramaic, a Chaldean language that replaced ancient Hebrew after the children of Israel were taken into captivity.

As a young boy, Paul learned the Old Testament law from the time he could hear and speak. His father certainly took Moses' instructions seriously which he gave to the children of Israel before they entered Canaan:

> *These commandments that I give you today are to be upon your hearts. Impress them on your children. Talk about them when you sit at home and when you walk along the road, when you lie down and when you get up. Tie them as symbols on your hands and bind them on your foreheads. Write them on the doorframes of your houses and on your gates. (Deut. 6:6–9)*

Paul would have committed to memory great sections of the Old Testament, devoting hours to listening, reading, and reciting the Targums, translations of the ancient Hebrew into either Aramaic or Greek. In fact, Paul probably memorized the Scriptures in both languages.

Studies with Gamaliel

When Paul reached his teen years (probably around thirteen or fourteen), he left Tarsus and traveled to Jerusalem where he studied to be a rabbi (see chronology chart on p. 6). His tutor was Gamaliel (Acts 22:3), a grandmaster who was greatly respected throughout the Jewish world. In the same address we looked at earlier, Paul told the Jerusalem audience he had been "brought up" in Jerusalem and "thoroughly trained in the law."

Gamaliel was also a member of the Sanhedrin, the ruling body in Jerusalem, comprised of the same men who sentenced

Stephen to death. However, it's doubtful that Gamaliel participated directly in this terrible act. On an earlier occasion when
these Jewish leaders had wanted to put the apostles to death,
Gamaliel had addressed them and warned them not to take such
action. "Leave these men alone! Let them go!" he had exhorted.
He reasoned that "if their purpose or activity is of human origin,
it will fail. But," he warned, "if it is from God, you will not be
able to stop these men; you will only find yourselves fighting
against God" (Acts 5:38–39). We can conjecture that he was
either overruled in the decision to stone Stephen, or he experienced a very dramatic change in his thinking. Both are possible
interpretations—as is the idea that he may have already died.

Paul learned most of his Jewish theology from Gamaliel.
Though as a young boy he was on his way to becoming a dedicated Pharisee while he still lived in Tarsus, he became a full-
fledged member of this group of men after learning at the feet
of Gamaliel. According to Josephus, the Pharisees numbered
about six thousand when Paul emerged as one of their zealous
leaders.[2]

F. F. Bruce outlines the way in which the Pharisees practiced their religion, which certainly would describe Paul in his
pre-conversion days:

> The Pharisees exercised great care in observing the Sabbath
> law and the food restrictions. . . . They scrupulously tithed the
> produce of the soil—not only grain, wine and oil, but garden
> herbs as well—and refused to eat food that was subject to the
> tithe unless the tithe had actually been paid on it. In their study
> of the law they built up a body of interpretation and application
> which in due course acquired a validity equal to that of the writ-
> ten law.[3]

This explanation helps us understand why Paul wrote to
the Philippians and stated that "in regard to the law," he was
"a Pharisee" and "as for legalistic righteousness, faultless"
(Phil. 3:5–6). He was dedicated to obeying every jot and tittle

of this written code. This is understandable since he firmly believed that he would obtain righteousness before God by keeping the law of Moses and the traditions of the elders. Consequently, when he joined this group, he was fully committed to the rigorous disciplines of this Jewish sect.

Ministry as a Rabbinical Pharisee

After his studies under Gamaliel, Paul eventually returned to Tarsus, probably five or six years after he arrived in Jerusalem. This would make him about eighteen or nineteen (see chronology chart on p. 6). We can only speculate regarding his activities in his home city for the next twelve to fourteen years. He evidently served as a rabbi in one of the local synagogues—perhaps a "Synagogue of the Freedmen." During this time, he certainly became exposed to a broader education in Greek and Roman culture. However, what he learned only made him a more zealous Pharisee.

Return to Jerusalem

After spending approximately fifteen years in Tarsus, this "young man named Saul" once again returned to Jerusalem. Since we are not told why, we can only speculate. However, we can assume he had received regular reports from his father and others who, as God-fearing Grecian Jews, made regular trips to the Holy City to worship in the temple. In fact, since he came from a wealthy family, both Paul and his father and other members of his family may have been visiting in Jerusalem on the Day of Pentecost when the Holy Spirit descended. But unlike thousands of other Jews—if they were there—they rejected Peter's message (Acts 2:41).

Whatever the actual facts, Paul had to have been terribly frustrated when he received reports about the growth of the church in Jerusalem. He became terribly angry at many of his fellow Jews for converting to Christianity. Furthermore, he had to have had some kind of ongoing connection with the

Sanhedrin to have emerged so quickly as the leader in the great persecution that followed Stephen's death. However, when the Holy Spirit inspired Luke to write a second letter to Theophilus (Acts 1:1), he did not think it was necessary for us to understand all of these details. Consequently, he simply recorded that those who stoned Stephen "laid their clothes at the feet of a young man named Saul." Thankfully, today we have much more information about Paul from the letters he wrote as a Christian which gives us a more complete and inspiring story. But before we continue to follow this exciting saga, let's pause to see what we can learn from this phase of Paul's life.

Becoming God's Man Today

Principles to Live By

Principle 1. It's possible to be intense and zealous about our religious and philosophical convictions but sincerely wrong (Gal. 1:13–14).

How well I remember, when as a relatively young man, I was asked to appear before a body of elders and ministers in my own denomination to give an account of why I had chosen to study at Moody Bible Institute and to fellowship with other people who claimed to be "Christians" but who were outside of our religious community. The meeting was held in the presence of hundreds of people in my own local church. Though I was given an opportunity to defend myself, in the end, I was excommunicated.

To this day, I have never questioned the sincerity of most of these people, many of whom are my blood relatives, others I still consider good friends. But needless to say, I still believe they were very confused theologically and definitely wrong in what they did.

What happened in my experience is not new in Christian history—beginning with the apostle Paul himself. After his conversion and his first missionary journey, he wrote to the

Galatians and described in graphic language his sincerity in practicing his religious beliefs:

> *For you have heard of my previous way of life in Judaism, how intensely I persecuted the church of God and tried to destroy it. I was advancing in Judaism beyond many Jews of my own age and was extremely zealous for the traditions of my fathers. (Gal. 1:13–14)*

Though most of us who grow up in a free society do not act on our own religious convictions to the same degree as Paul, we can become very opinionated about what we believe is truth. This often happens when we have been exposed to a certain belief system from childhood.

Remember also that Paul's attacks were not against the pagans in the Roman Empire but against his fellow Jews who departed from what he believed was the straight and narrow path. Just so, religious leaders today can become very hostile toward people who leave their fold. Sadly, many believe they are right, but like Paul, they're dead wrong!

Principle 2. It's possible to be very intelligent and knowledgeable about many things but also sincerely wrong (1 Cor. 2:1–5).

In his day, Paul was one of the most educated men in Jewish theology. Furthermore, he eventually became very astute in understanding Greek and Roman philosophy and literature. However, he was still blind to spiritual truth until he encountered Jesus Christ on the Damascus Road. The fact is, a well-rounded education can actually contribute to having a closed mind regarding God's revelation. The reason is simple. The more we learn, the more we can be in bondage to our own ego. Paul recognized this after his conversion when he wrote to the Corinthians that "knowledge puffs up" (1 Cor. 8:1).

Does this mean that all education is evil, as some religious groups believe? The answer is a decided no. In fact, we need more Christian scholars. But Paul warned against the negative influence of "human wisdom" (1 Cor. 2:12–13). James echoed this same concern when he wrote about "wisdom" that "is earthly, unspiritual" and even "of the devil" (James 3:15).

Even as dedicated believers, we must guard against developing blind spots because of the wisdom of this world. To steer clear of this pitfall, the answer is not to avoid a secular education but always to evaluate what we learn in the light of God's revealed wisdom in the Holy Scriptures. Learning will then become an exciting adventure.

This became true in my own studies at New York University where I earned a Ph.D. Though I had experienced some doubts earlier in my life, when I entered my doctoral studies in a secular university, I had become firmly convinced that any educational input that was not evaluated by the Word of God could become lethal in my life. When we make man the measure of all things—which secular education does—we're headed into a storm without a compass, without a map or a lighthouse to warn us of dangerous shoals. Furthermore, we don't have a firm destination. Paul used this metaphor to make a spiritual point when he wrote that some Christians "have shipwrecked their faith" (1 Tim. 1:19).

Paul also had some straightforward and enlightening words for non-Christians—something he could definitely identify with as he reflected on his own unconverted state of mind. Thus he wrote to the Corinthians: "The man without the Spirit does not accept the things that come from the Spirit of God, for they are foolishness to him, and he cannot understand them, because they are spiritually discerned" (1 Cor. 2:14).

This is why Paul, with all of his theological and philosophical knowledge, approached his audience with a spirit of humility and reliance on God. Thus he wrote to the Corinthians: "My message and my preaching were not with wise and persuasive words, but with a demonstration of the Spirit's power, so that your faith might not rest on men's wisdom, but on God's power" (1 Cor. 2:4–5).

Personalizing These Principles

Most of us have been exposed to religious beliefs and practices that need to be squared with the Word of God. Some of these ideas have little effect on our Christian lives since they are minor distortions which are eliminated as we grow in our knowledge of God's will as outlined in the Bible. However, some of these distortions can become serious roadblocks on our spiritual journey. This was certainly true in Paul's life—and in my own life as well.

The following questions will help you gain a clearer perspective regarding your theological viewpoints:

1. Do you really understand that the Bible teaches that salvation is a gift from God and cannot be earned by doing good works?

To answer this question, reflect on the following Scriptures. To make this an even more enlightening experience, take your Bible and read the context in which these verses appear:

- *For it is by grace you have been saved, through faith—and this not from yourselves, it is the gift of God—not by works, so that no one can boast. For we are God's workmanship, created in Christ Jesus to do good works, which God prepared in advance for us to do. (Eph. 2:8-10)*

- *Therefore, since we have been justified through faith, we have peace with God through our Lord Jesus Christ, through whom we have gained access by faith into this grace in which we now stand. And we rejoice in the hope of the glory of God. (Rom. 5:1–2)*

- *You are all sons of God through faith in Christ Jesus. (Gal. 3:26)*

- *For God so loved the world that he gave his one and only Son, that whoever believes in him shall not perish but have eternal life. (John 3:16)*

2. Is it possible that you are blinded and deceived by what you want to believe rather than what the Bible actually teaches?

A Project for Seekers

If you are attempting to discover who Jesus Christ really is, read John's Gospel with an open heart and mind. First, read John's purpose in writing this Gospel in John 20:30–31:

> *Jesus did many other miraculous signs in the presence of his disciples, which are not recorded in this book. But these are written that you may believe that Jesus is the Christ, the Son of God, and that by believing you may have life in his name.*

With this purpose clearly in mind, begin reading from the beginning of John's Gospel and try to discover how he attempted to achieve this purpose.

A Project for All Christians

To check out your own spiritual perspectives as a person who believes that Jesus Christ is the Son of God, try to eliminate all of your predisposed ideas about theology and read the Book of Ephesians. As you do, ask God to help you understand every aspect of this marvelous letter.

Set a Goal

As you reflect on Paul's experience as described in this chapter and as you review the "Principles to Live By," ask the Holy Spirit to reveal to you your most significant spiritual need. Then write out a specific goal for your life:

_____

_____

_____

_____

_____

Memorize the Following Scripture

Do your best to present yourself to God as one approved, a workman who does not need to be ashamed and who correctly handles the word of truth.
2 TIMOTHY 2:15

Growing Together

1. In what ways can you identify with Paul's experience when he was a non-Christian?
2. Would you share with us your personal spiritual journey to this point in your life?
3. As you reflect on the author's personal journey which he describes in the introduction to this book (see pp. 1–5), what one experience can you identify with the most? Would you explain why?
4. What can we pray for you specifically?

Chapter 2

A Supernatural Intervention

The term *intervention* has become a popular way to describe the process of confronting people we love—family members or friends who are heading in the wrong direction and who are on the verge of literally destroying their lives and desperately hurting those close to them.

Betty Ford, former first lady, serves as a classic example. She was an alcoholic and in extreme denial. Consequently, her husband, President Ford, and her family members confronted her. It was a painful encounter for everyone, but this intervention probably saved this woman's life. As a result, she acknowledged her alcoholism, went into treatment, and eventually founded the Betty Ford Clinic to help other people who have become addicted to alcohol and other chemical substances.

Paul's experience on the road to Damascus stands out as one of the most dramatic and significant interventions ever recorded. It was far more than human. In fact, it was a supernatural intervention by the Godhead—God the Father, Jesus Christ the Son, and the blessed Holy Spirit. Speaking directly from heaven, Jesus served as the divine spokesman for the Holy Trinity.

This supernatural intervention led to Paul's supernatural conversion. He was not simply delivered from an addiction, although he later described his attack on Christians as an "obsession." Rather, he "crossed over from death to life" (John 5:24). The natural intervention in Betty Ford's life may have delivered her, not only from her physical, psychological, and spiritual disease, but from an untimely *physical* death. However, the Lord's intervention in Paul's life delivered him from *eternal* death. As a Christian, Paul later spoke from personal experience when he wrote to the Romans: "For the wages of sin is death, but the gift of God is eternal life in Christ Jesus our Lord" (Rom. 6:23).

A "Holy Rampage" (Acts 8:1–3; 26:9–11)

Following his approval of Stephen's death, Paul immediately turned up the heat in his determination to stamp out Christianity. What began as a rather spontaneous act of hatred quickly evolved into a cruel, organized effort. Paul was on a "holy rampage"! His goal was "to destroy the church" (Acts 8:3). He literally went from "house to house" and hauled off to prison his fellow Jews who had put their faith in Jesus Christ as the Messiah.

I have used the term *holy* to describe this "great persecution." Though it was certainly evil and an act of hatred toward God Himself, Paul actually believed he was doing the Lord a great service. He was attempting to preserve the Mosaic Law and the sacred beliefs of Judaism.

Paul wasn't satisfied to restrict his vicious attacks on Christians to Jerusalem. Years later when he told his conversion story to Governor Festus and King Agrippa, he openly confessed his malicious and murderous activities:

> *On the authority of the chief priests I put many of the saints in prison, and when they were put to death, I cast my vote against them. Many a time I went from one synagogue to another to have them punished, and I tried to force them to blaspheme. In my obsession against them, I even went to foreign cities to persecute them. (Acts 26:10–11, author emphasis)*

Damascus was one of those foreign cities. Word had gotten back to Paul that some of the disciples of Christ who left

Jerusalem went to Damascus to escape his attacks. Consequently, he secured official documents from the high priest in Jerusalem to carry out his efforts in the synagogues and to bring these people back to face justice in Jerusalem (9:1–2).

Secular and religious history help us understand why Paul was able to get permission to carry out this kind of extradition within the Roman Empire. Rome had granted Judea the right to be a sovereign state and had given the high priest in Jerusalem the authority to pursue criminals who had left the area and to bring them back to Jerusalem to face punishment. Jews who had forsaken their religion to follow Jesus Christ were definitely considered worthy of imprisonment and even death. Their actions constituted a crime. This is why Paul had to secure permission from the high priest to carry out his mission.[1]

A Dramatic Conversion (Acts 9:3–9)

As noted by William James in his book entitled *The Varieties of Religious Experiences*, many people "outside of Christianity" have experienced unusual changes in their lives.[2] However, Christian conversion is unique in the way it is described in the Bible. It is not just a change of mind based upon a traumatic event, although it certainly may include these natural environmental and emotional dynamics. But when all is said and done, true Christian conversion is supernatural. Again and again, the Bible classifies this experience as passing from eternal death to eternal life. It is moving from darkness to light (1 Thess. 5:5). Jesus explained it as being "born again," not in a human sense, but as being regenerated by the Holy Spirit (John 3:3–9).

Three Detailed Accounts

The Lord definitely wanted us to know the specific details regarding Paul's conversion experience. That's why He inspired

Luke to give us three detailed accounts in the Book of Acts. The first account is the author's report. The second is Paul's first-person testimony before the Jews in Jerusalem years later. The third account is another first-person testimony as Paul spoke before Governor Felix and King Agrippa.

All of these events emphasized the same basic elements:

- Paul saw a brilliant light. (9:3; 22:6; 26:13)

- Paul was so stunned, he fell to the ground. (9:4; 22:7; 26:14)

- The risen and ascended Christ spoke directly to Paul and said, "Saul, Saul, why do you persecute me?" (9:4; 22:7; 26:14)

- Paul responded to this revelation with the words, "Who are you, Lord?" (9:5; 22:8; 26:15)

- Jesus responded to Paul's question by saying, "I am Jesus, whom you are persecuting." (9:5; 22:8; 26:15)

- Paul responded with a submissive question, "What shall I do, Lord?" (22:10)

- Jesus told Paul to arise and go into Damascus where he would receive further instructions. (9:6; 22:10; 26:16)

Paul's Born-Again Experience

When was Paul actually converted? It happened at that moment when this persecutor of Christians acknowledged that Jesus Christ was the Lord. This took place between the time he "fell to the ground" (9:4), heard Jesus' voice, and then cried out, "Who are you, Lord?" (9:5).

Paul was not simply using the word *Lord* as a courteous greeting. Rather, he was responding to Jesus Christ just as the blind man responded after he was healed and thrown out of the synagogue because he confronted the Pharisees (see John 9:1–38). Jesus found him and asked him, "Do you believe in the Son of

Man?" (9:35). At that moment, he had never met his "Healer" face to face, but he certainly recognized His voice. He already knew in his heart that Jesus was "from God" (9:33). Consequently, he asked, "Who is he, sir [or lord]?" He simply needed assurance that this was the man who had healed him and that He was also the One who claimed to be the Son of God. Jesus reassured him that He was the Savior, and at that moment the man who could now see physically had his eyes opened spiritually when he said, "Lord, I believe" and then "worshiped him" (9:38).

In essence, the same thing happened to Paul on the road to Damascus. Having fallen to the ground when he saw a bright light from heaven and having heard the voice of Jesus Christ, he asked, "Who are you, Lord?" Instinctively, he knew at that moment who Jesus Christ was, but he needed a confirmation. He received that confirmation when the Lord spoke once again and said, "I am Jesus, whom you are persecuting" (Acts 9:5). At that moment, Paul was born again. He knew and believed in his heart that Jesus Christ was the Messiah, the Son of God. He suddenly realized he had been resisting and fighting against the Lord. Through faith, that resistance suddenly disappeared, and he now understood that the conflict within his soul was the conviction of the Holy Spirit. Paul experienced true repentance and in the twinkling of an eye, he passed from death to life.

Physical Restoration

Though Paul's conversion experience was very similar to the blind man's that is described in John 9, his physical condition was reversed. Jesus first opened the eyes of the blind man and later opened his eyes spiritually. In Paul's case, Jesus first blinded his eyes physically and then opened the "eyes of his heart".

After Paul's dramatic conversion, the Lord told him to go into Damascus. There he would discover the next step he should take in his pilgrimage as a Christian. Paul obeyed and rose from the ground, and his traveling companions led him into the city. Luke has recorded that "for three days he was blind, and did not eat or drink anything" (9:9).

God had already been preparing a man in Damascus to minister to Paul. His name was Ananias. The Lord appeared to him in a vision and instructed him to "go to the house of Judas on Straight Street and ask for a man from Tarsus named Saul, for he is praying." The Lord told Ananias that He had already revealed to Paul that Ananias would "come and place his hands on him to restore his sight" (9:12).

Understandably, Ananias was anxious about this message. He had heard about Paul's murderous activities and that he had come to Damascus to arrest Christians and take them back to Jerusalem. But the Lord immediately put him at ease and told him that Paul was a "chosen instrument" to preach the gospel among the Gentiles. Ananias obeyed. When he arrived, he placed his hands on Paul and "immediately, something like scales fell from Saul's eyes, and he could see again" (9:18).

Baptismal Witness

The first thing Paul did following his physical healing was to be baptized. He had become a disciple three days earlier and now bore witness to his new life in Christ by obeying the command Jesus had given shortly before He returned to heaven. "Therefore go and make disciples of all nations," Jesus had said to his eleven disciples, "baptizing them in the name of the Father and of the Son and of the Holy Spirit" (Matt. 28:19).

It's important to note that Paul's baptism was not a part of his salvation experience. Rather, it was a result of this experience. He had already become a disciple of Christ on the road to Damascus when he acknowledged that Jesus Christ is Lord, the God who became flesh.

Either before or during or after his baptism in water, he was also "filled with the Holy Spirit" (Acts 9:17). Again, it's important to note that he had already been baptized into the body of Christ by the Holy Spirit when he believed in Jesus Christ

(1 Cor. 12:13). He was later "filled with the Holy Spirit" in preparation for the unique ministry God had called him to do—to proclaim the name of Jesus Christ "before the Gentiles and their kings and before the people of Israel" (Acts 9:15).

Jesus had commissioned Paul to this ministry moments after his conversion on the road to Damascus. Years later, he shared these details when he stood before King Agrippa. Jesus had spelled out his calling after Paul had asked the question "Who are you, Lord?" Following is Jesus' very descriptive reply:

> *I am Jesus, whom you are persecuting . . . Now get up and stand on your feet. I have appeared to you to appoint you as a servant and as a witness of what you have seen of me and what I will show you. I will rescue you from your own people and from the Gentiles. I am sending you to them to open their eyes and turn them from darkness to light, and from the power of Satan to God, so that they may receive forgiveness of sins and a place among those who are sanctified by faith in me. (Acts 26:15–18)*

Evidence That Demands a Verdict

There is no way to deny that something unusual happened to Paul on the road to Damascus. Secular historians acknowledge this dramatic event and even liberal theologians who deny that there are miracles confess that they know something very unusual happened. However, they try to explain it in natural terms. For example, some say Paul had a seizure which threw him to the ground. Others believe he might have been a victim of a sunstroke, which is why he saw such a bright light. However, if these theories are true, isn't it amazing what kind of changes took place in this man as a result of a seizure or a sunstroke?

Before and After

- Before his conversion, Paul hated the name of Jesus; afterward, he revered His name.

- Before, Paul hated those who followed Jesus Christ; afterward, he became a dedicated follower himself.

- Before, Paul had Christians imprisoned and some murdered; afterward, he was persecuted for his own faith in Christ and eventually went to prison and became a martyr like Stephen—the man he condemned to death.

- Before, Paul was on a mission to stamp out the Christian message; afterward, he devoted his life to preaching that same message.

- Before, Paul proclaimed that the way of righteousness was to keep the law of Moses; afterward, he proclaimed the message of salvation by grace.

- Before, Paul was motivated to serve God out of fear and anger; afterward, he served God out of love and appreciation for God's grace.

Seizures and sunstrokes do not change a person like Paul was changed. Rather, he experienced a supernatural encounter with the living Christ that day on the Damascus Road. His life was dramatically changed with the power of the Holy Spirit. This was no human intervention—as helpful as that can be. This was a supernatural experience with God Himself. Paul was born again. His transformation is unequalled in the history of Christianity.

Holy Spirit Conviction

When Paul shared his testimony before King Agrippa and related Christ's words—"Saul, Saul, why do you persecute me?"—he included a statement from the Lord that is omitted in the other two accounts. Jesus also said, "It is hard for you to kick against the goads" (compare 26:14 with 9:4, 22:7), which raises at least two important questions.

- First, what did Jesus mean?

- Second, why did Paul include this statement in his testimony before King Agrippa?

To answer the first question, we need to understand the term *goads*. These were sharp sticks that were used to prod animals. Applied to Paul's experience, Jesus must have been referring to the convicting power of the Holy Spirit. In other words, what would appear to be a hard, calloused conscience was in actuality a sensitive but confused heart. Though Paul was obsessed with the task of stamping out Christianity, there were certain scenes he certainly could never remove from his mind. How could he forget the supernatural expression on Stephen's face when he spoke before the Sanhedrin? Luke has recorded that these men, which certainly included Paul, "looked intently at Stephen, and they saw that his face was like the face of an angel" (6:15).

Furthermore, how could Paul forget that incredible scene when "Stephen, full of the Holy Spirit, looked up to heaven and saw the glory of God, and Jesus standing at the right hand of God"? Try as he might, he could never ignore Stephen's words—"I see heaven open and the Son of Man standing at the right hand of God" (7:55–56). And when Paul saw a light from heaven and heard Jesus' voice—"Saul, Saul, why do you persecute me?"—he could not have ignored Stephen's testmony that day as he saw the son of Man standing at the right side of God.

Even more convicting, Paul certainly could never forget Stephen's prayer as he fell to his knees while he was being pelted with stones: "Lord, do not hold this sin against them" (7:60).

In moments of aloneness, these words coming from the heart of a bruised and bleeding man must have rung in Paul's ears. Though he continued on his "holy rampage," he was kicking "against the goads." Like an animal who is being prodded, the Holy Spirit kept urging Paul to listen to his conscience. But he ignored the Lord's voice and persisted in his attacks on the followers of Jesus Christ.

And then it happened. Because Paul was acting in ignorance and unbelief, God had mercy on him. Even though he was "a blasphemer and a persecutor and a violent man," Jesus Christ intervened in his life (1 Tim. 1:13–14).

But why did Paul include this metaphor in his testimony before Agrippa? I believe Paul was saying to the king what Jesus Christ had said to him on the road to Damascus: "It is hard for you to kick against the goads." Paul knew Agrippa's background and his knowledge of Old Testament history. He also knew that Agrippa was aware of the Christian movement. This is why he responded to Governor Festus—who interrupted his testimony and accused him of losing his mind because of his extensive education—and said:

> *"I am not insane, most excellent Festus," Paul replied. "What I am saying is true and reasonable. The king is familiar with these things, and I can speak freely to him. I am convinced that none of this has escaped his notice, because it was not done in a corner. King Agrippa, do you believe the prophets? I know you do." (Acts 26:25–27)*

King Agrippa responded to Paul's question in what appears to be a defensive fashion: "Do you think that in such a short time you can persuade me to be a Christian?" (26:28). The facts seem to be that the Holy Spirit was prodding Agrippa's heart, and Paul knew it. He was encouraging this man to stop resisting the truth and to believe in Jesus Christ and be born again. In other words, Paul was encouraging Agrippa to avoid the "ignorance and unbelief" that had led to his own resistance to the Christian message.

Unfortunately, King Agrippa did not respond to the gospel, at least at this time, even though he could not ignore Paul's change of heart. However, he acknowledged that Paul was innocent of the charges against him and would have set him free "if he had not appealed to Caesar" (26:32). More importantly, I personally believe Agrippa also knew that Paul was right about Jesus Christ—that He was the promised Messiah, the Savior of the world.

Becoming God's Man Today

Principles to Live By

Principle 1. God wants all people to acknowledge their sins and to believe that the Lord Jesus Christ is the Son of God and to receive Him personally and be saved.

After Paul had devoted a number of years to preaching to both Jews and Gentiles the good news that Jesus Christ had died and rose again, he wrote a letter to the Christians in Rome. He stated that we "all have sinned and fall short of the glory of God" (Rom. 3:23). He also wrote that "the wages of sin is death" (6:23). However, Paul was quick to assure his readers—and us—that "the gift of God is eternal life in Christ Jesus our Lord."

How do we receive this gift and avoid "the wages of sin"? Paul answered this question clearly in a very dramatic scene on his second missionary journey when he and Silas were ministering in Philippi. Both of them had been incarcerated for preaching the gospel. In fact, they were severely beaten and placed in a section of the prison reserved for hardened criminals.

In spite of their suffering, these two ambassadors for Jesus Christ began to pray and to sing hymns. Luke has reported that it was "about midnight" when "suddenly there was such a violent earthquake that the foundations of the prison were shaken." The doors of the prison were jarred loose and "flew open." At the same time, "everybody's chains came loose" (Acts 16:25–26).

It doesn't take much imagination to reconstruct what happened in the heart and mind of the jailer when he suddenly awakened and discovered what had happened. He knew that life would be over for him when his superiors found out that all of the prisoners had fled. Consequently, he "was about to kill himself."

Paul saw what was happening and shouted, "Don't harm yourself! We are all here!" (16:28). The jailer was stunned and overwhelmed. He quickly called for torches so that he could see. Guiding Paul and Silas out of the prison, he asked the most important question any man can ask in a lifetime: "Sirs, what must I do to be saved?" (16:30).

In the midst of this incredible scene, Paul and Silas answered this question with the most wonderful words anyone could ever utter: "Believe in the Lord Jesus Christ, and you will be saved" (16:31). The man responded in faith and passed from eternal death into eternal life.

This is what happened to the blind man who met Jesus on the outskirts of Jerusalem. This is also what happened to Paul on the road to Damascus. This is what God wants for every human being who is ever born into this world. As the apostle Peter has reminded us: "The Lord . . . is patient" with all of us, "not wanting anyone to perish, but everyone to come to repentance" (2 Peter 3:9).

Principle 2. God wants all people who believe in Jesus Christ to be baptized in order to bear witness that they have died with Christ and have risen to a new life.

After Paul and Silas had shared the gospel with the Philippian jailer, he invited them into his private dwelling. He gently and compassionately washed the blood and grime from their bruised and bleeding backs and bound up their wounds. He then invited these two godly men to share the same good news with his whole family. Obviously, Paul and Silas shared that the promise of eternal life included the jailer's whole family if they too would believe in the Lord Jesus Christ. They responded in faith, received God's gift of salvation, and then were baptized (Acts 16:33).

Again, it should be noted that "baptism in water" followed their baptism by the Holy Spirit into the body of Jesus Christ. However, all of those who were old enough to understand and personally believe were baptized with water following their conversion experience. Once again, Paul and Silas were simply carrying out the Great Commission of our Lord

Jesus Christ. Water baptism was designed by God to be an outward symbol of an inward reality. The inward reality is that by faith we can die with Christ, be buried with Him, and be raised to a new life—and even be seated with Christ in heavenly realms (Eph. 2:1–10). The outward symbol simply illustrates what has already happened in our hearts. Going into the water symbolizes death, and rising from the water symbolizes our resurrection and new life in Jesus Christ.

Principle 3. God wants all people to respond to the convicting ministry of the Holy Spirit.

Jesus Christ sent the Holy Spirit into the world to "convict the world of guilt in regard to sin and righteousness and judgment" (John 16:7–8). The more we resist Him, the more He lovingly prods us to respond to the truth.

I remember so well my own conversion. Two of my best friends had responded to the gospel. But I resisted! I knew the truth but wanted to live life my way. However, the more I resisted, the more the Holy Spirit tugged at my heart and convicted me of my sin. In fact, I was so miserable I couldn't enjoy life the way I wanted to live it. Finally, I gave in, fell to my knees, confessed my sins, and received the Lord Jesus Christ as my Savior. It was then I began to experience peace. I began to experience God's "good, pleasing and perfect will" (Rom. 12:2).

Personalizing These Principles

Reflect on the following words penned by the apostle John:

> And this is the testimony: God has given us eternal life, and this life is in his Son. He who has the Son has life; he who does not have the Son of God does not have life. I write these things to you who believe in the name of the Son of God so that you may know that you have eternal life. (1 John 5:11–13)

If you should die this very moment, are you sure of where you would spend eternity? Don't resist the convicting ministry of the Holy Spirit. If you cannot say with confidence that you *know* that you have eternal life, take the following steps and you can be sure:

1. Have you acknowledged that you are a sinner—that you have fallen short of God's perfect standard?
2. Do you understand and accept the fact that the Lord Jesus Christ is the Son of God and that He died in your place on the cross and paid for the wages of sin, which is eternal death?
3. Have you received this gift of eternal life by believing in the death and resurrection of Jesus Christ for you personally?
4. If you haven't taken these steps, won't you do so today? You will experience a supernatural conversion—just like the blind man, just like Paul, and just like the Philippian jailer and his family.

   Don't expect the emotional dynamics described in these New Testament experiences to be the same as yours. However, what happens in your life will be the same supernatural event.
5. Have you been baptized in water since you've become a Christian?

   To be baptized is to be obedient to the command of Jesus Christ. Once we become disciples, we are to demonstrate to others with baptism that we have died with Christ and have been resurrected to a new life. Even though we are saved by grace through faith, God wants us to be a witness in this world. One very significant way that He has planned for this to happen is for Christians to be baptized.

Set a Goal

As you reflect on Paul's conversion and the principles that flow from his Damascus Road experience, ask the Holy Spirit

to pinpoint a need in your own life. Then set one specific goal
you want to reach:

_____

_____

_____

_____

Memorize the Following Scripture

> For it is by grace you have been saved, through faith—
> and this not from yourselves, it is the gift of God—not by works,
> so that no one can boast. For we are God's workmanship,
> created in Christ Jesus to do good works,
> which God prepared in advance for us to do.
> Ephesians 2:8–10

Growing Together

1. Would you share with us when you were saved and how
   this changed your life?
2. To what extent did you resist the message of salvation and
   experience the convicting ministry of the Holy Spirit?
3. Why is it important not to attempt to equate our conversion experience in every detail with that of the apostle
   Paul?
4. What is your view of baptism and how does it compare
   with what we've studied in this chapter?
5. Why is it important to understand that water baptism
   should come after our salvation experience?
6. What can we pray for you specifically?

Chapter 3

An Unequaled Transformation

Conversion followed by transformation is the essence of biblical Christianity. However, the changes that happen in people's lives vary greatly. For example, my wife, Elaine, has a difficult time even identifying a moment in time when she was converted. However, she does remember that as a little girl about age eight she read a story about a young boy who had put his faith in the Lord Jesus Christ for salvation. His parents died, and because of his faith, he was able to share his eternal hope with the doctors and nurses in the hospital.

This simple, true-to-life story touched Elaine's young heart. She realized that she had done things that displeased God, and she knew that she needed to be saved. Though details are vague, she traces her conversion to this experience. It was not dramatic from an emotional point of view, and there were no great outward changes in her little eight-year-old life. But from an eternal point of view, it was definitely a life-changing event.

On the other end of the continuum, we have examples of more dramatic conversions. For example, Chuck Colson, former assistant to Richard Nixon, quickly became known in Washington as a "hatchet man"—one who did the "President's dirty work." In fact, an unnamed author of an article in the *Wall Street Journal* stated that "Colson would walk over his own grandmother if he had to in order to achieve his self-oriented goals." Someone else accused him of being "tough, wily, nasty and tenaciously loyal to Richard Nixon."[1]

But then came another headline a couple of years later in the midst of the Watergate scandal: "Colson makes decision for Christ." Most everyone in Washington was startled and suspicious. Could this be? Is it a gimmick? A personal ploy to seek leniency for Colson's involvement in Watergate? Even the Christian community was skeptical. Yet, Charles Colson's conversion was real. He had become a born-again believer, and his life was dramatically changed.

Few Human Comparisons

Though Colson's experience and others like his have certainly been dramatic, Paul's encounter with Jesus Christ stands out above all others. He is definitely on the opposite end of the continuum from child conversions such as my wife Elaine's experience. He was a grown man and a zealous Jew who hated the gospel that was being preached by first-century Christians. He approved of Stephen's death by stoning and continued to persecute and incarcerate his fellow Jews who had put their faith in Jesus Christ as the promised Messiah (Acts 8:1–3).

But then it happened! He met the resurrected and ascended Christ on the road to Damascus. He was on his way with authorized permission from the high priest in Jerusalem to arrest both men and women who had become Christians and to bring them back to Jerusalem as prisoners (Acts 9:1–9).

There are a number of synonyms that could be used to describe Paul's transformation—graphic, moving, touching, powerful, striking, spectacular. It certainly was stirring and even electrifying for those Jews who had already accepted Jesus as the Christ or Messiah. On the other hand, Paul's transformation was definitely unnerving and threatening for those unbelieving Jews who witnessed what had happened. They were mystified. How could this be? Their leader had suddenly become a turncoat.

From Persecutor to Preacher (Acts 9:19–22)

After Jesus appeared to Paul, Paul experienced blindness for three days (Acts 9:9). Could it be that this period of darkness symbolizes the three days the Savior spent in the tomb? And could it be that when Paul's eyes were miraculously opened, it was symbolic of Christ's resurrection? Whatever the Lord had in mind for Paul, no one can deny that his three days without sight set the stage for one of the most remarkable and momentous "new-life" transformations of all time. Though he was instantaneously converted and born again the moment he acknowledged Jesus as Lord (Acts 9:5), Paul then began to experience extraordinary changes in his thoughts, attitudes, and actions.

Paul's born-again experience was indeed life-changing, not only in terms of his eternal destiny but in terms of his present behavior. During the few days he stayed in Damascus, "he began to preach in the synagogues that Jesus is the Son of God" (9:20). Those who knew why he had come to Damascus in the first place "were astonished." They couldn't believe their ears. Again and again people who heard Paul's message asked the same questions: "Isn't he the man who raised havoc in Jerusalem among those who call on this name [that is, the name of Christ]? And hasn't he come here to take them as prisoners to the chief priests?" (9:21).

Paul's new message is what made his transformation so startling. Before he was converted, he rejected the essence of Christianity altogether—that God became a man. But once he understood who Jesus really was, he not only personalized this truth in his own life, but he began to preach a message that was diametrically opposed to what he had previously believed. And what made this transformation even more startling is that before he became a Christian, he not only rejected the message of Christ but imprisoned and murdered many of his fellow Jews who had received the Lord Jesus Christ as their personal Savior.

From Obtrusiveness to Obscurity (Gal. 1:11–17)

Luke's Succinct Biographical Account

When Luke recorded Paul's story, he succinctly condensed what happened. In fact, there seems to be a lengthy period of time between Acts 9:21 and 9:22.[2] After Paul "at once began to preach in the synagogue that Jesus is the Son of God," amazing "all those who heard him" and provoking the questions we noted earlier, Luke went on to record that Paul "grew more and more powerful and baffled the Jews living in Damascus by proving that Jesus is the Christ" (9:22).

A quick glance at Luke's account makes it appear that this transition from *preaching* that Jesus was the Son of God to *proving* He was the Christ happened immediately. In reality, there seems to be at least a two- or three-year time gap between these two events. In the days following his conversion, Paul was clearly not yet ready for this kind of intense apologetic ministry. He was a new believer and an infant Christian, spiritually and emotionally. Consequently, after the "several days" of preaching mentioned by Luke, he left Damascus and spent time in Arabia learning—and unlearning—many things (see chronology chart on p. 6).

Paul's Enlarged Autobiographical Account

Paul himself helps us understand this time gap. A number of years after his initial experience in Damascus, he wrote a letter to the Galatian Christians, believers he and Barnabas had led to Christ on their first missionary journey:

> For you have heard of my previous way of life in Judaism, how intensely I persecuted the church of God and tried to destroy it. I was advancing in Judaism beyond many Jews of my own age and was extremely zealous for the traditions of my fathers. But when God, who set me apart from birth and called me by his grace, was pleased to

reveal his Son in me so that I might preach him among the Gentiles
[Luke described this conversion in Acts 9:1–19], I did not consult any
man, nor did I go up to Jerusalem to see those who were apostles before
I was, but I went immediately into Arabia [after Acts 9:21] and later
returned to Damascus [see Acts 9:22]. (Gal. 1:13–17) [3]

Paul's statement that he went "immediately into Arabia"
correlates with Luke's reference to the "several days" he spent
with the disciples in Damascus (Acts 9:19). Evidently, he then
left the city unhindered.

Paul's personal account in no way detracts from Luke's
credibility as a historian or from the fact that the Holy Spirit
inspired him to record this event accurately. The Lord simply
led him to do what many of us do in relating historical events.
In order to make "a long story short," we eliminate certain
details but at the same time tell exactly what happened.

For example, if someone wrote my biography, he might
say—very accurately: "Gene graduated from Moody Bible
Institute in Chicago. He then joined the faculty as a professor.
However, he eventually moved to Dallas and started the first
Fellowship Bible Church."

All of these statements are true; however, what the person
writing this biographical sketch didn't tell you is that I spent
two years in Billings, Montana, *after* graduating from Moody
Bible Institute. It was there I received a college degree. Furthermore, he didn't tell you I moved back to the Chicago area
and entered the Graduate School at Wheaton College and
while completing my Master's degree, I "then joined" the
Moody faculty. He also failed to tell you that while I taught at
Moody, I spent nine summers completing my doctoral degree
at New York University. And he didn't tell you that when I
moved to Dallas, I became a member of the Dallas Seminary
faculty, where I served for five years *before* I "started the first
Fellowship Bible Church."

In essence, Luke did the same thing when he recorded
Paul's story. He intentionally left out some events in Paul's

personal journey in order to condense the historical account. However, Paul himself later described his personal history in more detail when he wrote several of his letters. As we've noted, this is particularly true when he wrote his letter to the Galatians.

From Law to Grace (Exod. 20:1–17)

At Mount Sinai

We are not sure where Paul actually lived in Arabia. Some believe that it was in the same vicinity where Moses received the Ten Commandments and other laws and regulations from the Lord at Mount Sinai. If this is an accurate interpretation, it gives us a fascinating correlation between Paul's experience and what happened to Moses in this very area centuries before.

After Moses had delivered the children of Israel from Egypt, God led them to the foot of this holy mountain. It was there Moses received the moral and civil laws. It doesn't seem coincidental that the Lord may have led Paul to Mount Sinai to reveal to him—not His laws—but the gospel of His grace.

This was a revolutionary message for Paul. All his life he had believed he could earn righteousness and salvation by keeping legalistic rules. Reflecting on this experience, he confessed to the Philippian Christians that he had "put confidence in the flesh," that "in regard to the law," he was a dedicated "Pharisee," and "as for legalistic righteousness," he was "faultless" (Phil. 3:4–6). Though he certainly began to understand salvation by grace the moment he was converted on the Damascus Road, he came into a much fuller understanding of this wonderful truth while in Arabia. This is why he also wrote to the Galatians using a "prison" metaphor to describe our relationship to the law compared with our freedom in Christ when our faith unlocks the doors that keep us in bondage: "Before this faith came, we were held prisoners by the law, locked up until faith should be revealed. So the law was put in charge to lead us to Christ that we might be justified by faith. Now that faith has come, we are no longer under the supervision of the law" (Gal. 3:23–25).

In view of Paul's calling to preach the message he had once denied, it's logical, therefore, to conclude that God would lead him back to the place where the law was originally given in order to help him understand grace.

A Direct Revelation

If Paul received God's message of grace at Mt. Sinai, we see another correlation. Just as Moses received the Old Testament message (law) *directly from God,* so Paul received the New Testament message (grace) *directly from God.* Again, Paul describes this experience in his letter to the Galatians: "I want you to know, brothers, that the gospel I preached is not something that man made up. I did not receive it from any man, nor was I taught it; rather, I received it by revelation from Jesus Christ" (Gal. 1:11–12).

Paul was not saying that he was the only one who had received this kind of truth. Rather, he was reporting that Jesus Christ revealed the gospel to him before he had consulted other New Testament leaders (1:16–17). As we'll see, his conversations later with Peter and the other apostles in Jerusalem only confirmed that his experiences were real and valid—which leads to another insight that became clearer to Paul during this obscure period of his life.

From Rabbi to Apostle (1 Cor. 15:3–10)

During his stay in Arabia, Paul also began to understand clearly his apostolic role. However, his calling to be an apostle differed greatly from the other men outlined in Scripture as "apostles of Jesus Christ." These twelve men spent three and a half years following Jesus Christ while He traveled throughout Galilee and Judea. They heard Jesus teach that He was the true

Messiah and Savior of the world and that this salvation came through faith, not the law (John 3:16). They saw Him work miracles to prove His deity (John 20:31) and witnessed His death and resurrection. Before He ascended, they heard Jesus proclaim the Great Commission to make disciples of all nations (Matt 28:19–20). They then witnessed the powerful coming of the Holy Spirit in Jerusalem and experienced the spectacular birth of the church (Acts 2:1–11).

Paul, on the other hand, received his divine call to be an apostle after Christ had returned to heaven and after the Holy Spirit had come on the Day of Pentecost. In fact, the church had multiplied phenomenally, involving thousands of believers (Acts 2:41; 4:4).

Paul never fully understood God's mercy and grace in calling him to the same high position held by the other apostles, especially in view of his hatred toward those who believed in Jesus Christ. Consequently, he wrote to the Corinthians: "For I am the least of the apostles and do not even deserve to be called an apostle, because I persecuted the church of God. But by the grace of God I am what I am, and his grace to me was not without effect. No, I worked harder than all of them—yet not I, but the grace of God that was with me" (1 Cor. 15:9–10).

In spite of his unworthy feelings, Paul knew beyond a shadow of a doubt that Jesus Christ had called him to be an apostle. Writing to Timothy, he said without equivocation:

> For there is one God and one mediator between God and men, the man Christ Jesus, who gave himself as a ransom for all men—the testimony given in its proper time. And for this purpose I was appointed a herald and an apostle—I am telling the truth, I am not lying—and a teacher of the true faith to the Gentiles. (1 Tim. 2:5–7)

Paul not only believed he had this special calling because of what Jesus revealed to him directly, but also because of the special gifts he received from Jesus Christ (Eph. 4:11–12). In defending his apostleship to the Corinthians, he reminded them that "the things that mark an apostle—signs, wonders and miracles—were done among you with great perseverance" (2 Cor. 12:12). No one could deny that Paul had a unique and special calling—just like Peter and the other men who were taught directly by Christ and given the same powerful spiritual gifts to verify this calling (Heb. 2:3–4).

From Israel to the Church (Eph. 3:2–12)

There is one other major truth Paul certainly must have learned for the first time during his stay in Arabia. In his letter to the Ephesians, he called it the "mystery of Christ" (Eph 3:4). In essence, he was speaking of the church (Eph. 3:10), which he often described as "the body of Christ." Interestingly, Paul was the only New Testament writer who used this very descriptive metaphor.

All of his early life, Paul believed he had a corner on God's promises because he was an Israelite. He had little use for Gentiles and believed they were outside of God's earthly and eternal plan. But while in Arabia, God revealed His wonderful design regarding the church. More specifically, Paul learned that "this mystery is that through the gospel the Gentiles are heirs together with Israel, members together of one body, and sharers together in the promise in Christ Jesus" (Eph. 3:6).

Again, Paul did not claim to be the only one to understand this mystery. Thus he wrote that "it has now been revealed by the Spirit to God's holy apostles and prophets" (3:5). However, Paul once again learned this truth—not from other men—but directly from Jesus Christ. This is why he stated: "Surely you have heard about the administration of God's grace that was given to me for you, that is, the mystery made known to me by revelation" (3:2–3).

This statement also correlates with what Paul wrote to the Galatians when he said, "I did not receive it [the gospel] from any man, nor was I taught it; rather, I received it by revelation from Jesus Christ" (Gal. 1:12). This gospel not only involved the message regarding the Lord's death, burial, and resurrection (1 Cor. 15:3) but also that all who believe this message become one in Christ. Thus he also wrote: "You are all sons of God through faith in Christ Jesus, for all of you who were baptized into Christ have clothed yourselves with Christ. There is neither Jew nor Greek, slave nor free, male nor female, for you are all one in Christ Jesus" (Gal. 3:26–28).

Becoming God's Man Today

Principles to Live By

Paul's conversion and transformation are examples for all Christians. Though few people, if any, will ever be able to identify with the intense drama and miraculous aspects of his calling and life changes, we can identify with the supernatural aspects of the new birth and the transforming power of Jesus Christ.

Principle 1. Once we are converted (born-again) through faith in Christ, it is God's will that we all be transformed into His image.

Paul made this point very clear when he wrote to the Roman Christians. After describing in great detail God's love and grace in providing a way to be saved from our sins (Rom. 3:23; 6:23) and to be made righteous through faith in Jesus Christ (Rom. 5:1), he appealed to all of us as believers to present our bodies to God "as living sacrifices," which we can do through the power of the Holy Spirit (8:1–2). He went on to exhort us not to "conform any longer to the pattern of this world." Rather he said, "Be transformed by the renewing of your mind" (Rom. 12:1–2). In other words, we should allow Christ to live His life through us.

Paul's exhortation to "be transformed" is based on God's mercy. He is asking us to allow "the grace of God" to motivate us "to live self-controlled, upright and godly lives"

(Titus 2:11–12). Since we are free in Christ, we are not to use our "freedom to indulge the sinful nature." Instead, we are to "serve one another in love" (Gal. 5:13). In other words, if we "live by the Spirit," we "will not gratify the desires of the sinful nature" (5:16).

Paul outlined the same process of transformation in his letter to the Ephesians. As new believers, we are "to be made new in the attitude of" our "minds." We are "to put off" our "old self" and "to put on the new self, created to be like God in true righteousness and holiness" (Eph. 4:22–24).

This transformation should be evident in every true Christian's life. However, there will be a great deal of diversity in our various experiences—which leads us to our next principle.

Principle 2. Though it is God's will that all of us as Christians be transformed by the renewing of our minds, this process varies depending on our individual backgrounds.

When some people are born again, the change that takes place in their lives is hardly noticeable. They have been reared in a Christian home, have ordered their lives according to biblical values, and simply move on to a new and deeper relationship with God. They haven't been drug addicts, lived immoral lives, or committed murder. Like Timothy, they "have known the holy Scriptures" from the time they could hear and understand (2 Tim. 3:15). And when they are old enough to comprehend that they have sinned and fallen short of God's eternal glory, they have put their faith in Jesus Christ and experienced salvation.

In some respects, this describes Paul before he became a Christian. He too had learned the Holy Scriptures from early childhood. He had devoted his life to keeping the law of Moses. However, rather than accepting Jesus Christ as the Son of God and Savior of the world as Timothy did, he had become angry, rejected the Christian message, and tried to destroy those who became disciples. But when he met the risen and ascended

Christ on the Damascus Road, he did an about-face. He immediately started proclaiming a message he had previously hated. This is what made his transformation so dramatic.

Augustine

Throughout church history, there are some people who have experienced this kind of dramatic change in their lives after they have become Christians. Consider Augustine who wrote the classic book *The City of God*. When he was thirty-two years old, he sat in the garden of a friend. He had tears running down his cheeks. Though he had a good job as a professor of rhetoric, he was under deep conviction from the sins in his life. He wanted to forsake this old lifestyle but couldn't break away from his lustful patterns.

While wallowing in his feelings of guilt and shame, Augustine heard a child singing the words "Take up and read! Take up and read!" At the same time, he noticed a scroll by his side. Picking it up and flipping through it, his eyes fell on the words of Paul in the letter to the Romans:

> The night is nearly over; the day is almost here. So let us put aside the deeds of darkness and put on the armor of light. Let us behave decently, as in the daytime, not in orgies and drunkenness, not in sexual immorality and debauchery, not in dissension and jealousy. Rather, clothe yourselves with the Lord Jesus Christ, and do not think about how to gratify the desires of the sinful nature. (13:12–14)

The Holy Spirit used these statements by Paul to penetrate Augustine's heart and to bring him to personal faith in Christ. It became his "Damascus Road" experience. Later he wrote, "No further would I read, nor had I any need; instantly . . . a clear light flooded my heart, and all the darkness of doubt vanished away."

Augustine was not only converted but his lifestyle was transformed. Some have identified him as "the greatest Christian since New Testament times." F. F. Bruce has written that this change in lifestyle "can be traced directly to the light which flooded into his mind as he read the words of Paul."[4]

Martin Luther

Martin Luther is another example. He was an Augustinian monk and served as professor of sacred theology in the University of Wittenberg. While preparing lectures on the Psalms, Luther was agonizing over God's righteousness. He felt condemned. While he was reflecting on his sorrowful state, his eyes also fell on Paul's words to the Romans: "For in the gospel a righteousness from God is revealed, a righteousness that is by faith from first to last, just as it is written: 'The righteous will live by faith'" (Rom. 1:17).

Luther later wrote:

> I had greatly longed to understand Paul's epistle to the Romans, and nothing stood in the way but that one expression, "the righteousness of God," because I took it to mean that righteousness whereby God is righteous and acts righteously in punishing the unrighteous . . . and night and day I pondered until . . . I grasped the truth that the righteousness of God is that righteousness whereby, through grace and sure of mercy, He justifies us by faith.
>
> Therefore I felt myself to be reborn. I have gone through open doors into paradise. The whole of Scripture took on a new meaning, and whereas before "the righteousness of God" had filled me with hate, now it became to me an inexpressibly sweet and greater love. This passage of Paul became to me a gateway into heaven.

The end of this story is dramatic. Luther became a great leader in launching a spiritual reformation that changed the world. Like Paul, his new theological insights transformed his own life and the lives of millions of people.

This process of transformation in the lives of these men continued for a lifetime—as it does in all of our lives. Again, some changes happen quickly. Some take more time. For the apostle Peter, it took five years and a vision from heaven to enable him to overcome his prejudice against Gentiles. In fact, he didn't even believe that Gentiles could be saved during this period of time following the launching of the church at Pentecost. Following the conversion of Cornelius and those in his household, he confessed: "I now realize how true it is that God does not show favoritism but accepts men from every nation who fear him and do what is right" (Acts 10:34–35).

A Personal Experience

I think of my own conversion. I was saved at age sixteen. However, I had been reared in a religious community where I was taught we were the only ones who had the truth. Furthermore, I had been taught a list of legalistic rules which were essential for my salvation to be complete.

Needless to say, I struggled with emotional turmoil for several years. Ironically, like Peter, it also took me at least five years to overcome my prejudice which had been built into my life from childhood. In this sense, I can identify somewhat with both Paul and Peter. However, when I understood salvation by grace through faith, the process of transformation began to happen more quickly. Though it took time to overcome the feelings that accompanied my theological confusion, I soon began to experience true freedom in Jesus Christ.

Personalizing These Principles

After Paul exhorted the Ephesians to "put off the old self" and "to put on the new self," he outlined some specific things that should happen. Read the following exhortations and check those areas that need some special attention in your own life:

- *Therefore each of you must put off falsehood and speak truthfully to his neighbor, for we are all members of one body. (Eph. 4:25)*

- *In your anger do not sin: Do not let the sun go down while you are still angry, and do not give the devil a foothold. (4:26–27)*

- *He who has been stealing must steal no longer, but must work, doing something useful with his own hands, that he may have something to share with those in need. (4:28)*

- *Do not let any unwholesome talk come out of your mouths, but only what is helpful for building others up according to their needs, that it may benefit those who listen. (4:29)*

- *And do not grieve the Holy Spirit of God, with whom you were sealed for the day of redemption. (4:30)*

- *Get rid of all bitterness, rage and anger, brawling and slander, along with every form of malice. (4:31)*

- *Be kind and compassionate to one another, forgiving each other, just as in Christ God forgave you. (4:32)*

- *But among you there must not be even a hint of sexual immorality, or of any kind of impurity, or of greed, because these are improper for God's holy people. (5:3)*

- *Nor should there be obscenity, foolish talk or coarse joking, which are out of place, but rather thanksgiving. (5:4)*

Set a Goal

As you reflect on the principles outlined in this chapter as well as Paul's exhortations in his letter to the Ephesians, ask the Holy Spirit to show you one goal you need to set for your life in order to become more conformed to the image of Jesus Christ:

_____

_____

_____

_____

_____

Memorize the Following Scripture

Therefore, I urge you, brothers, in view of God's mercy, to offer your bodies as living sacrifices, holy and pleasing to God—this is your spiritual act of worship. Do not conform any longer to the pattern of this world, but be transformed by the renewing of your mind. Then you will be able to test and approve what God's will is—his good, pleasing and perfect will.
ROMANS 12:1–2

Growing Together

1. Would you share your own conversion experience?
2. Would you share how your life has been transformed since you've become a Christian? In other words, what changes have taken place in your life?
3. Which of the following men do you identify with the most in terms of their new life in Christ: The apostle Paul, Timothy, Augustine, Martin Luther, the author?
4. What changes would you like to see take place in your life?
5. What can we pray for you specifically?

Chapter 4

A Friendship Is Born

When Paul became a Christian, he began a new life, not only in terms of what he believed but in terms of who believed in him. As a rabbinical Pharisee he was highly respected, not only in his own hometown but in the heartland of Judaism. His closest friends were devout religious leaders who were adamantly opposed to Christianity. He was totally trusted by the seventy-one men who formed the most powerful ruling body in Judaism, the Sanhedrin. The high priest had even entrusted Paul with the responsibility to round up Jewish Christians and to bring them back to Jerusalem for punishment.

All of that changed abruptly when Paul became a Christian. Not only was he rejected by the majority of his own people, but those who had become Christians in Jerusalem prior to Paul's conversion did not believe that he was truly one of them. His behavior had been so malicious toward believers that they would not risk any kind of association with Paul.

However, God had a plan to help Paul become accepted in the Christian community, particularly when he returned to Jerusalem after his three-year stay in Arabia. It all began with one man who took time to get to know him, befriend him, and then build a bridge to the apostles. But this is getting ahead of the story.

Old Truth but New Meaning (Acts 9:22–25)

When Paul returned to Damascus from Arabia, he once again used the synagogue as a platform to preach the gospel (see chronology chart on p. 6). A couple of years before, just after he had been converted, he "astonished" his fellow Jews by preaching a message he had vehemently denied: "that Jesus is the Son of God" (Acts 9:20). But three years later, he had grown substantially in his Christian faith. His message had deepened. He was definitely more theologically astute. Though his encounter with the resurrected and ascended Christ on his first journey to Damascus had convinced him that Jesus was who He claimed to be—God's only begotten Son (John 3:16)—he now was able to prove from Scripture "that Jesus is the Christ," the promised Messiah (Acts 9:22).

During Paul's stay in Arabia, God spoke to him directly, revealing the true nature of the gospel of grace (Gal. 1:11–12) and that all who believe this good news—whether Jew or Gentile—become one body in Christ (Eph. 3:4–6). But Paul certainly must have spent hours reflecting on what he had already learned from the Old Testament revelation prior to his conversion. His fertile mind was filled with biblical truths that he had learned at his father's knee and in the synagogue school in Tarsus. Furthermore, his years of pouring over "the law and the prophets" as he studied under Gamaliel in Jerusalem became both the seedbed and foundation for fully understanding God's covenant with Abraham. More importantly than God's promise to give this Old Testament patriarch the land of Canaan and to make him into "a great nation" was the promise to bless all people on earth through the Messiah who would eventually appear, not only as a future son of Abraham, but as the Son of God (Gen. 12:1–3).

Paul quickly began to see the history of his own people through different eyes. His three days of blindness and the scales that fell from his eyes when Ananias prayed for him in Damascus served as a continuous and symbolic reminder of an ongoing process that would change his life forever. All that he had learned from the Scriptures began to come alive with new meaning. That Jesus was the promised Messiah was the most life-changing truth of all.

The Suffering Messiah

As the Lord renewed Paul's mind, he began to see the Messianic prophecies in the Old Testament with an entirely new perspective. He was well aware of the promises that the Messiah would come to rule and reign as King in Israel, but at the same time he virtually blocked out the promises that this same Messiah would suffer before he came to earth to be a sovereign ruler. For example, David's Messianic Psalms certainly took on this new meaning for Paul in view of what he now knew about Christ's death and resurrection. He now understood that King David was speaking of the suffering Messiah, not of himself.

David's Prophetic Voice

Following are some of David's Psalms that certainly revolutionized Paul's perspectives about the Messiah—many of which were fulfilled at the cross:

Old Testament Messianic Prophecies	New Testament Fulfillment
Psalm 22:1	Matthew 27:46
My God, my God, why have you forsaken me?	*My God, my God, why have you forsaken me?*
Why are you so far from saving me, so far from the words of my groaning?	(See also Mark 15:34)
Psalm 22:18	Matthew 27:35
They divide my garments among them and cast lots for my clothing.	*When they had crucified him, they divided up his clothes by casting lots.*
	(See also Mark 15:24; Luke 23:34; John 19:23–24)

Psalm 27:12
*Do not turn me over to the
desire of my foes,
for false witnesses rise up
against me, breathing out
violence.*

Matthew 26:59–60
*The chief priests and the
whole Sanhedrin were
looking for false evidence
against Jesus so that they
could put him to death. But
they did not find any,
though many false witnesses
came forward.*
(See also Mark 14:56)

Psalm 31:5
*Into your hands I commit my
spirit; redeem me, O LORD,
the God of truth.*

Luke 23:46
*Jesus called out with a loud
voice, "Father, into your
hands I commit my spirit."
When he had said this, he
breathed his last.*

Psalm 41:9
*Even my close friend, whom I
trusted, he who shared my
bread, has lifted up his heel
against me.*

Matthew 26:23
*Jesus replied, "The one who
has dipped his hand into
the bowl with me will
betray me."*
(See also Mark 14:20–21;
Luke 22:19–23; John
13:26–30)

Psalm 69:21
*They put gall in my food and
gave me vinegar for my
thirst.*

Matthew 27:34
*There they offered Jesus wine
to drink, mixed with gall;
but after tasting it, he
refused to drink it.*
(See also Mark 15:36)

Isaiah's Powerful Words

The Book of Isaiah must have become one of Paul's
favorite prophetic treatises. But imagine how he felt the first
time he really understood the prophecies regarding Christ's

suffering. We can be sure that Jesus' question from heaven—
"Saul, Saul, why do you persecute me?"—never vanished from
his mind. He began to see his part not only in nailing Christ to
the cross but in continuing to persecute Jesus by attacking the
members of His glorious body, the church. With this new perspective, Paul must have often wept both tears of remorse and
joy as Isaiah's words pierced his heart:

> *He was despised and rejected by men,*
> > *a man of sorrows, and familiar with suffering.*
> *Like one from whom men hide their faces*
> > *he was despised, and we esteemed him not.*
> *Surely he took up our infirmities*
> > *and carried our sorrows,*
> *yet we considered him stricken by God,*
> > *smitten by him, and afflicted.*
> *But he was pierced for our transgressions,*
> > *he was crushed for our iniquities;*
> *the punishment that brought us peace was upon him,*
> > *and by his wounds we are healed.*
> *We all, like sheep, have gone astray,*
> > *each of us has turned to his own way;*
> *and the* LORD *has laid on him*
> > *the iniquity of us all. (Isa. 53:3–6)*

Paul must have asked himself many times why he hadn't
understood these words before. Then too, how often he must
have reflected on that terrible scene in Jerusalem when he had
orchestrated Stephen's death because he had accused the leaders in Israel of rejecting the Messiah. On the other hand, this
terrible experience only intensified his burden to communicate the true message, first of all, to his fellow Jews. Consequently, when he returned to Damascus, he preached with
deep passion, intense conviction, and depth of insight. Thus
Luke has recorded: "Yet Saul grew more and more powerful
and baffled the Jews living in Damascus by proving that Jesus
is the Christ" (Acts 9:22).

Resistance to the Messianic Message

Paul's Old Testament expositions created a lot of turmoil and confusion among his fellow Jews. The message was both one of hope and condemnation—hope for those who believed and received forgiveness, and condemnation for those who rejected their Messiah. When they refused to repent and believe, they only added to their national sin as God's chosen people who had orchestrated the crucifixion.

Was Paul surprised initially when both he and his message were rejected by his own people? Perhaps. But it should have been expected in view of Paul's own pre-conversion behavior. It's not surprising, however, that he thought he could convince them to avoid his stubborn unbelief and horrible mistakes. But he was naïve at first. We are not told how soon he understood Israel's terrible spiritual blindness because of their sins (Rom. 11:25), but he was soon to find out—beginning in Damascus.

A Deliberate Conspiracy

We're not sure how much time passed before the Jews actually came up with a specific plan to kill Paul. Luke simply recorded that "many days had gone by" before "the Jews conspired to kill him" (Acts 9:23). However, we do know that the Greek words and construction in the original text indicate a duration of time, perhaps several months. Though their death strategy gradually emerged, the Jews' anger and frustration certainly began to build immediately when Paul began to confront them outright with their sin of rebellion.

Political Considerations

Though it's clearly recorded that the Jews were the ones who conspired to kill Paul, they did not have the authority to capture him and sentence him to death. Years later, Paul added more important details. Writing to the Corinthians, he informed them that his fellow Jews secured the cooperation of the local authorities, who in turn took the responsibility to capture Paul. He wrote:

> *In Damascus the governor under King Aretas had the city of the Damascenes guarded in order to arrest me. But I was lowered in a basket from a window in the wall and slipped through his hands. (2 Cor. 11:32–33)*

Damascus was ruled by a governor who had been appointed by King Aretas, who ruled over an Arabic tribe known as the Nabataeans. These people were raw pagans who worshiped a variety of gods. We're not sure of the governor's ethnic background, but we can be sure that he was not enamored with either the Jewish religion or Christianity. However, he cooperated with Paul's enemies in their conspiracy. This is why it must have taken time for the Jews to orchestrate this plot. They did not have the same political power as members of the Sanhedrin did in Jerusalem who conspired to kill Stephen. In that case, the Roman government had given these high-powered men the authority to enforce their own Jewish laws in matters related to the religion. Not so in Damascus![1]

Faithful Followers

Fortunately, Paul had developed a lot of friends in Damascus, especially among his fellow Christians. Furthermore, there were probably some prominent Jews who had not yet believed the gospel but who were sympathetic to Paul's message. In a sense, they would be like Nicodemus, a member of the Sanhedrin in Jerusalem, who secretly approached Jesus during the night and indicated that he didn't share the same attitudes as his Jewish colleagues on the ruling council (John 3:1–2).

Whatever the source, Paul "learned of the plan" and went into hiding. Furthermore, his loyal followers devised a scheme to help him escape. One of the disciples obviously had a home built on the wall that surrounded the city with a window facing outward. They secured a large basket and, with ropes, lowered Paul to the ground, enabling him to escape without harm (Acts 9:25).

Distrust and Fear in Jerusalem (Acts 9:26–29)

Paul immediately made his way back to Jerusalem, probably taking the same route he had traveled three years earlier on his way to Damascus to take Christians prisoner (see chronology chart on p. 6). No doubt feeling a deep sense of rejection and aloneness, he knew the time had come to return to the Holy City. Paul later wrote that his primary purpose in going to Jerusalem was "to get acquainted with Peter" (Gal. 1:18), the leader of the apostles and a man he had once hated. He may have begun to experience some doubts about his own calling and mission—particularly in view of the conspiracy to kill him—and needed reassurance that he was indeed called to be an apostle.

But Paul was in for a surprise. Even after three years, the followers of Jesus Christ were still afraid of him. They had obviously heard about his conversion but were understandably skeptical. After all, this zealous Pharisee had imprisoned many disciples and had approved of a number of deaths. Some of these people were probably still behind bars. And you can imagine what Stephen's friends thought when word got out that Paul had returned. A lifetime would not have blurred their memories regarding that horrible experience. Consequently, it's not surprising that Christians in Jerusalem wondered if Paul's return and claim to be a believer was some type of insidious plot to infiltrate their community and then once again precipitate an all-out war against the church.

Barnabas—Son of Encouragement

Before Paul met Peter, he was destined to meet another man who would become a true friend and eventually a fellow missionary. When the disciples refused to believe that Paul was a true Christian, Barnabas walked onstage in this dramatic scene and intervened for Paul. In fact, he arranged for him to meet with the apostles, although we know from Paul's autobiographical account in his letter to the Galatians that only Peter was available, along with James, the Lord's brother (Gal. 1:18–19).

Barnabas's sudden appearance raises some interesting questions:

- How and where did he meet Paul?

- Why did he believe in Paul when everyone else distrusted him?

- Why was he willing to take this risk?

An Exploding Church

To answer these questions, let's review who Barnabas was. He first appeared several years before when the church was growing and expanding by leaps and bounds. The Grecian Jews who had come to Jerusalem from all over the Roman world to attend the feast of Pentecost and then became Christians on the last day—"the day of Pentecost" (Acts 2:1–41)—decided to stay and wait for the next chapter in God's unfolding mystery. Since there were thousands who made this choice, it created a serious need for room and board. Consequently, "from time to time those who owned lands or houses sold them," and then "brought the money from the sales and put it at the apostles' feet, and it was distributed to anyone as he had need" (Acts 4:34–35).

A Businessman from Cyprus

It's at this point that we first meet Barnabas. His original name was Joseph and he was from the island of Cyprus. This means he was also a Grecian Jew. Either he had permanently moved to Jerusalem or he traveled back and forth from his own country in order to develop and oversee a thriving real estate business.

Whatever the circumstances, Joseph had become a Christian and joined the thousands of other believers as "they devoted themselves to the apostles' teaching and to the fellowship, to the breaking of bread and to prayer" (Acts 2:42). When challenged by the physical needs of his fellow Grecian Jews, he "sold a field he owned and brought the money and put it at the apostles' feet" (4:37). At this point, we learn something very significant about Joseph. Before he had actually engaged in this wonderful act of generosity, the apostles had already changed his name to Barnabas, "which means Son of Encouragement" (4:36).

There is only one reason why this happened. Barnabas was what his name states—an encourager. Furthermore, the Holy Spirit wants Christians of all time to know that his encouraging personality was directly related to his generous spirit. That's why we learn about his name change in the context of helping to meet the physical needs of his fellow Christians. He was an unselfish and caring man. This helps explain why he took time to get acquainted with Paul.

Aunt Mary and Cousin Mark

Jumping ahead in the biblical timeline, we know that a number of believers often met in the home of a woman named Mary (Acts 12:12). We also know that this Mary was the mother of John Mark, a young man who later joined Paul on his first missionary journey (13:5) and eventually wrote one of the four Gospels. Furthermore, we know that Mark was a cousin of Barnabas (Col. 4:10). In view of these family relationships, it's logical to conclude that Barnabas had been staying (or at least visiting) at his aunt's home. And since this was a very popular place for Christians to meet on a regular basis, it's logical to conclude that Paul would in some way end up knocking on the "outer" entrance to Mary's home (Acts 12:13).

Suppose for a moment that Paul did knock at Mary's door. Imagine that it was the servant girl Rhoda who first heard Paul identify himself on the outside of the outer entrance (12:12–13). If so, we can imagine her surprise and fear as she left Paul standing—like she would do some time later to Peter (12:14)—and reported this shocking information to her mistress. After all, three years earlier, Paul and his anti-Christian compatriots had appeared at the doors of many homes—probably Mary's door as well—and forced their entrance and hauled off disciples and imprisoned them. No believer who was in Jerusalem at that time would have forgotten those horrible days.

A Listening Ear

Whatever the circumstances, Barnabas found out quickly about Paul's sudden return to Jerusalem and took time to meet with him face-to-face. We can assume that they had never met before, either before Paul's conversion or afterwards, but we can also assume that Barnabas certainly was aware of who Paul was and what he had done to Stephen and to other believers in Jerusalem.

When Barnabas interfaced with him, he must have listened intently as Paul shared his conversion story. He would also have listened carefully to what happened in Damascus—the first time as well as the second time—and what happened during Paul's years in Arabia. Though we're not told specifically what transpired in this meeting, we can say with certainty that Barnabas believed that Paul was for real. A deep friendship was born, and this meeting between these two men was destined to change the course of history. It was indeed a "watershed" moment in Paul's life. He learned how much he needed someone to help him bear the burden in ministry.

Barnabas Intercedes for Paul

Convinced of Paul's unique calling, Barnabas built a bridge for Paul to the apostles. Though only Peter and James, the Lord's brother, were available to meet with them, Barnabas shared what he had learned and believed. Three facts stand out in his communication. First, "he told them how Saul on his journey had seen the Lord." Second, he told them "that the Lord had spoken to him." And third, he shared "how in Damascus he had preached fearlessly in the name of Jesus" (Acts 9:27).

In this brief historical account, we have additional reasons why Barnabas was an encourager. Not only was he unselfish and generous with his material possessions, but he believed in people. More importantly, he took time to get to know people so he could believe in them. And he was also willing to take a risk with his trust. His encounter with Paul illustrates all of these qualities.

Think for a moment how risky it really was for Barnabas to intercede for Paul before Peter and James. Here was a man who had been a ruthless murderer. What if this was a plot—a feigned conversion—in order to do serious harm to the primary leaders of the church? The results would have been disastrous. But Barnabas was willing to take that risk. He firmly believed Paul's testimony. Furthermore, we cannot overlook the fact that Barnabas walked so closely with God that the Holy Spirit certainly bore witness with his own spirit that Paul was indeed telling the truth.

A Bridge Is Built

These mediating efforts paid off. Peter and James also believed God had worked a miracle in Paul's life. Luke recorded that Paul "stayed with them and moved about freely in Jerusalem, speaking boldly in the name of the Lord" (9:28). In other words, once Peter and James trusted Paul, their trust opened the door for other Christians to trust him too.

Though Paul was only in Jerusalem for a relatively short time, he took advantage of the opportunity. In addition to spending quality time with Peter and James, he "talked and debated with the Grecian Jews" (9:29). How ironic! These are no doubt some of the very same men who had confronted

Stephen and argued against his message (6:9–14). And now the very man who had bought into their lies and orchestrated Stephen's death stood face-to-face with these men arguing for the very message he once tried to destroy. Even more ironic, these Grecian Jews became so agitated and angry, "they tried to kill" Paul—just as they had successfully done to Stephen (9:23).

Back Home Again (Acts 9:30–31)

Because of the intense hostility, Paul's visit to Jerusalem was cut short.[2] He was soon on his way to Caesarea and then back to Tarsus, his home city. Once again Paul had faced persecution and suffering, but once again he was delivered. Some of the loyal Christian brothers in Jerusalem found out about the plot and quickly ushered him out of Jerusalem. Like Barnabas, they too were willing to take a risk. They now knew beyond a shadow of a doubt that Paul's conversion was authentic. He was a transformed man.

This ended an era of persecution against Christians. Even though Paul had launched this terrible harassment over three years earlier, it had continued after he became a Christian. However, when he left Jerusalem the second time, for some unstated reason, the ill treatment subsided. Luke has recorded:

> *Then the church throughout Judea, Galilee and Samaria enjoyed a time of peace. It was strengthened; and encouraged by the Holy Spirit, it grew in numbers, living in the fear of the Lord. (9:31)*

Becoming God's Man Today

Principles to Live By

The principles I've chosen to emphasize in this phase of Paul's life actually focus on Barnabas and his relationship with Paul. Humanly speaking, without Barnabas, Paul would never have gotten a hearing in Jerusalem.

Principle 1. There are times when all of us need a "Barnabas" in our lives—someone who believes in us when we may not even believe in ourselves.

When Paul returned to Damascus and then to Jerusalem, he quickly learned how much he needed people in his life. More specifically, he needed a "Barnabas"—someone who would believe in him and build bridges to other people.

I remember when I first entered Moody Bible Institute as a student. Along with the other freshman, I was asked to take an entrance exam in composition. I flunked it! I couldn't even finish the sentence "I came to Moody Bible Institute because . . . ." Needless to say, I had to take remedial composition. Even then, I had a difficult time expressing myself in writing.

As I look back, it's hard to believe that I have become an author, having written nearly fifty books. However, there is a reason. When I didn't believe in myself, God brought into my life a professor who saw potential in me. In fact, he encouraged me to go on to college after I graduated from Moody Bible Institute with the thought in mind of returning to Moody as a teacher in his department.

When Dr. Harold Garner first suggested that idea, it went in one ear and out the other. Again, I couldn't imagine myself instructing others. He never let me forget that he believed I could do it. It seems amazing now, but I did come back and join the faculty as one of the youngest men who had ever held this kind of position. I was only twenty-three years old when I began to teach college students.

Again, there's a reason. This man believed in me when I didn't believe in myself. Furthermore, he was willing to take a risk and represent me to others. He did for me what I could not do for myself, just as Barnabas did for Paul when he returned to Jerusalem. I'll be forever grateful!

Principle 2. God wants all of us to be "encouragers," people who are generous with our time, talent, and treasures—people who are willing to get involved in others' lives, even willing to take a risk.

When Paul wrote to the Thessalonians, he stated two times that we are to encourage one another and build each other up (1 Thess. 4:18; 5:11). Barnabas definitely illustrated how we can do this:

- We encourage others when we share our material possessions generously and unselfishly.

- We encourage others when we use our talents and abilities to build up other members of the body of Jesus Christ.

- We encourage others when we are available, using our time, to get to know others and to meet needs in their lives.

Barnabas illustrated all three of these qualities and, as a pastor, I know from experience how encouraging people like this can be. They're the brothers and sisters who "come alongside" with their time, talents, and treasures and help me bear the burdens of ministry. Without them, I would not be able to carry on.

As a husband, I also know how important these qualities are in my wife. Over the years, she has been my encourager. She's unselfish with our material possessions. In fact, when we got married, she taught me to tithe—to give at least ten percent of my income to the Lord's work. In addition, in spite of the incredible demands of motherhood, she has always made me and my ministry a priority in her life. Again, I'll be eternally grateful. There were days when I would have given up without her love and support.

And then one of the greatest sources of encouragement has come in recent years from my adult children. They've all honored me and shared words of encouragement—on many occasions. But I remember one event particularly. As a pastor, I was under severe attack from several very sinful men, one of whom is still in prison for a serious moral crime. My adult daughter voluntarily defended my character publicly. Another daughter wrote me a letter from college—one I still cherish. She told me how I had always represented Jesus to her. Her words of encouragement helped me face this crisis victoriously and without compromising what I knew to be true.

Personalizing These Principles

1. How have you expressed appreciation to the encouragers in your life?

    Most of us have had men who have served in the Barnabas role in our lives, even though we may have forgotten or taken them for granted. I've seen young men who have been trusted and discipled by others. In many instances, they have gotten unique opportunities for ministry because their mentors opened doors they couldn't open themselves. Sadly, I've seen these very same men as they became successful never look back over their shoulders. In fact, they have given the appearance they accomplished their goals all by themselves. How tragic! This is a reflection of selfishness and arrogance. Never forget your Barnabas!

2. How does your personality pattern help you or hinder you in being an encourager?

    It's true that many of us are designed by God from birth to be different personalities. Some of us are highly relational and love to be with people. Encouraging others comes naturally. Others of us are less relational and feel more comfortable with projects than people. In these instances, it takes more effort and determination to reach out to others. But remember that when we walk in the Spirit and allow God to control our lives, we are able to love others supernaturally in ways that are beyond our natural abilities. Paul demonstrated this reality in a marvelous way. He was a very tough-minded man who became a gentle warrior.

Set a Goal

As you review the principles in this chapter, ask the Holy Spirit to reveal one area in your life that needs immediate attention. Then set a specific goal, asking God to enable you to achieve that goal:

_____

_____

_____

_____

Memorize the Following Scripture

*And let us consider how we may spur one another on toward
love and good deeds. Let us not give up meeting together,
as some are in the habit of doing, but let us encourage one another—
and all the more as you see the Day approaching.*
HEBREWS 10:24–25

Growing Together

1. Can you name another Christian who has served in a special way as a Barnabas in your life? Why has this been true?
2. In what ways are you serving as a Barnabas in someone else's life? If you don't have this kind of relationship with someone, can you think of someone you would like to serve in this way?
3. In what ways does your God-created design help you to be a Barnabas? In what ways does this design seem to hinder you? If you feel frustrated, could it be that your God-created design has been distorted because of unfortunate and environmental circumstances?
4. How has your conversion to Jesus Christ and your relationship with Him impacted your desire to be a Barnabas?
5. What can we pray for you specifically?

Chapter 5

Rejected at Home

*O*ver the years, I've counseled many Christians who have an intense burden to reach their parents and other close relatives with the gospel. With few exceptions, they have experienced rejection when they've tried to share this message of hope. In fact, the very day I penned these words, I received an e-mail from a man in our church who requested prayer for an unsaved relative who was seriously ill. However, his prayer request focused more on this person's spiritual condition than her physical well-being. He was hoping to be able to share the gospel.

I immediately picked up the phone and called my friend in order to get more information. During the conversation about his seriously ill aunt, we also talked about his parents who were both religious but also non-Christians.

"Have you tried to share the gospel with them?" I asked.

"Yes," he replied, "but the last time I tried to explain the message of salvation with my dad, he got so angry that he asked me to leave the house." Though his mother was not quite as overt in her rejection, she shared her husband's sentiments.

As we concluded the conversation, I prayed for my friend and his loved ones that he might be able to share the gospel openly but sensitively—and without experiencing alienation. However, we both recognized that there might be more rejection.

As I reflected on this experience, I thought of Paul when he had returned to Tarsus—now as a Christian. It was a traumatic experience. He also suffered some painful rejection from those he had been close to. However, this was not a surprise for Paul.

"He Must Suffer for My Name"

From the time Paul became a Christian, he knew—at least generally—what lay ahead. The Lord made this clear to Ananias in Damascus when He instructed him to look for Paul and to lay his hands on him. When Ananias hesitated because of Paul's murderous reputation, the Lord responded, "Go! This man is my chosen instrument to carry my name before the Gentiles and their kings and before the people of Israel. I will show him how much he must *suffer for my name*" (Acts 9:15–16).

We're not told everything Ananias shared with Paul after he could see again, but we can be certain he relayed these prophetic words. Consequently, the persecution Paul faced when he returned to his home city, Tarsus—this time as a Christian—did not catch him totally off guard.

In some respects, Paul had already experienced this kind of rejection when he had returned to Damascus from Arabia and "the Jews conspired to kill him" (9:23). The same thing happened again when he returned to Jerusalem where he had previously distinguished himself as a great Jewish scholar. When he entered the Holy City as a Christian, those who knew him best, the Grecian Jews, also "tried to kill him" (9:29).

These murderous plots were only the beginning of a life of suffering for Paul. The Damascus and Jerusalem experiences would fade in his memory compared with the ongoing persecution he would receive in Tarsus where he had spent his pre-teen years as well as his subsequent years as a distinguished Jewish leader.

Putting the Pieces Together

To understand what happened when Paul returned to Tarsus as a Christian, we must remember his first return to his home city as a zealous Jew. After he had studied the traditions of Pharisaic Judaism in Jerusalem under Gamaliel, he came back to his roots. He no doubt took up the tentmaking trade he had learned as a young boy, and at the same time served as a young, august rabbi, teaching in many of the Jewish synagogues that were scattered throughout the city. It was during this period that people came to know him best as a "Hebrew of Hebrews" and a dedicated Pharisee (Phil. 3:5).

Paul spent approximately twelve to fourteen years in Tarsus, but following Christ's death, resurrection, and ascension, he once again returned to Jerusalem. It was then he approved of Stephen's death and launched the persecution against the church. In the midst of this onslaught against Christians, he was converted on the Damascus Road, spent three years in Arabia, and then returned to Damascus and to Jerusalem to preach the message he had once denied. It was at this point, following the threats on his life, that "the brothers . . . took him down to Caesarea and sent him off to Tarsus" (Acts 9:30), where he once again lived for a period of six to eight years. This time, however, he proclaimed the gospel of Jesus Christ, informing his Jewish family and friends that he had personally met the Messiah (see chronology chart on p. 6).

With this brief reference to Paul's return to Tarsus (9:30), Luke virtually bypassed this important period of Paul's life as a Christian. Evidently, the Holy Spirit wants us to learn what happened in Tarsus directly from Paul's pen. After all, a first-person report can be far more impacting than a third-person account. This is what we'll see when we eventually look at several references in his second letter to the Corinthians.

Disappointed but Obedient

As a firm believer that Jesus Christ was the promised Messiah, Paul left Jerusalem aware that his message had been rejected by the Grecian Jews. Though he certainly was terribly disappointed, the Lord had spoken directly to Paul at some point during this brief witnessing opportunity, directing him to leave as soon as possible.

Years later, Paul stood before a hostile and violent mob after returning from his productive missionary journeys and addressed his fellow Jews in Aramaic, their common language. He explained what had happened after he had left Damascus and had come back to Jerusalem as a Christian: "'When I returned to Jerusalem and was praying at the temple, I fell into a trance and saw the Lord speaking. "Quick!" he said to me. "Leave Jerusalem immediately, because they will not accept your testimony about me"'" (Acts 22:17).

Paul's response to the Lord's directive to leave Jerusalem indicates his keen disappointment. He felt a deep sense of responsibility to correct his fellow Jews' theological perspective on Jesus Christ. At that moment, he reminded the Lord that in his unconverted days, he had gone "from one synagogue to another to imprison and beat those who" had believed in Jesus Christ. And what bothered him the most was that he had approved of Stephen's death (22:19–20). Obviously, that's why he had "talked and debated with the Grecian Jews" (9:29). He wanted to convince those who had set Stephen up for martyrdom that they were terribly deluded, just as he had been (6:8–9).

In spite of Paul's person-to-person dialogue with Jesus Christ as he expressed his sense of obligation to his own people, the Lord insisted that he leave Jerusalem and go "far away to the Gentiles" (22:21). His work was basically finished in the Holy City. As much as he wanted to correct what he had so sadly misinterpreted in his unconverted days, Paul needed to accept the fact that those in Jerusalem had been given a greater opportunity to believe the gospel than any other group of people on earth. After all, Jesus Christ was crucified and resurrected in Jerusalem. It was there He had appeared to a number of people and then returned to heaven. It was there He had sent the Holy Spirit to give birth to the church. It was there that the apostles—Peter and John particularly—had preached and worked miracles, demonstrating that Jesus Christ was indeed who He claimed to be. It was there many thousands of Jews had put their faith in the Messiah and had proclaimed the gospel to their friends and neighbors. In essence, the Lord was telling Paul that the Jews in Jerusalem and the surrounding area had had their chance. It was now time to carry the message to those who had not heard a clear presentation of the gospel, including Jews, but particularly Gentiles.

"No Prophet Is Accepted in His Hometown"

As stated earlier, one of the most difficult places to share the message of salvation is among those who know us best. This should not surprise us since Jesus Christ faced this dilemma when He returned to Nazareth, also His own hometown. When He claimed to be the anointed prophet and preacher mentioned by Isaiah, His own fellow Nazarenes bitterly rejected Him. Though they were initially impressed with His wisdom and "the gracious words that came from his lips" (Luke 4:22), they eventually turned against Him—particularly when He challenged their faith as Jews and commended the Gentiles for their response to spiritual truth (Luke 4:25–30). They actually became so angry that they tried to throw him over a cliff. In the midst of all this turmoil, Jesus made a powerful statement, identifying with Elijah and Elisha in their prophetic ministry in Israel. "'I tell you the truth,' he continued, 'no prophet is accepted in his hometown'" (Luke 4:24). And when Paul returned to Tarsus, he eventually faced this same kind of rejection. Jesus' prophecy came true in his own experience.

Paul's parents, relatives, fellow rabbis—and the whole Jewish community—were in for the shock of their lives. The young man they had been so proud of because of his religious "zeal" (Phil. 3:6) had done an about-face. The Jesus he had detested had become the motivating force in his life. Though they had certainly heard about his conversion to Christianity, they could not have predicted the 180-degree change in his life and the extent of his redirected zeal.

Parental Rejection

Think for a moment how Paul's return to Tarsus affected his parents. What had happened to this little newborn son they were so proud of when they had him "circumcised on the eighth day" (Phil. 3:5)? What had so dramatically changed this bright youngster who had learned the Jewish traditions at his father's knee and had memorized the Torah in synagogue school? And what about his incomparable education in Jerusalem? After all, it cost his father dearly to send his young son to the Holy City to study under one of the greatest Jewish scholars in the world.

Obviously, Paul's parents would not understand how their son could renounce his Jewish faith and become a Christian. Furthermore, the shame and embarrassment would be almost more than they could bear. And what would make their pain even more difficult was that they had only two choices as dedicated Jews—to follow their son's example, accept Jesus as the Messiah, and be alienated by the Jewish community, or to reject this message and disown and disinherit Paul as their son. This kind of parental rejection was more than social. It was also financial. His father, who was obviously a very wealthy man, would cut him off from the family fortune.

Paul certainly knew what might happen when he shared his Damascus Road experience with his parents, yet he certainly hoped and prayed that they would respond to the gospel. However, there is no biblical evidence they ever did. Perhaps he could still see their negative reactions—anguish, fear, anger, and resentment—as he years later penned his letter to the Romans and said: "I have great sorrow and unceasing anguish in my heart. For I could wish that I myself were cursed and cut off from Christ for the sake of my brothers, those of my own race" (Rom. 9:2–3).

As Paul wrote these words regarding his fellow Jews, his parents and immediate family would certainly have been at the forefront of his mind.

Marital Separation

What about Paul's marital status? Did he ever have a wife? Some believe he did. According to the rabbis, every dedicated Jewish father had three goals in regard to his son. First, he wanted him to learn the Old Testament laws and the traditions of Israel. Second, he wanted to teach him a trade—a way to make a living. Third, he wanted to help him secure a good wife.

Paul's father certainly wanted to achieve all three of these goals. However, we only know for sure that he achieved two of them. First, Paul definitely received an unequaled Jewish heritage in terms of religious beliefs, and, second, he became very skilled as a tentmaker. But was he married?

Some Bible teachers speculate that Paul was alluding to his own experience when he wrote his first letter to the Corinthians and addressed the subject of separation and divorce. Note the following directives:

> *If any brother has a wife who is not a believer and she is willing to live with him, he must not divorce her. And if a woman has a husband who is not a believer and he is willing to live with her, she must not divorce him. . . . But if the unbeliever leaves, let him do so. A believing man or woman is not bound in such circumstances; God has called us to live in peace. (1 Cor. 7:12–13, 15)*

If Paul did have a wife, she either died or refused to believe the gospel her husband had been called to preach. But if she had died, why wouldn't Paul have mentioned her? More likely she chose to leave the marriage. This may have been one of the most painful prices Paul paid because of his faith in Jesus Christ. But if this happened—even though Paul taught that a Christian "is not bound in such circumstances"—he never remarried. He devoted all of his efforts to proclaiming the message of salvation.

Religious Persecution

Though it would be terribly painful emotionally for Paul to be rejected by members of his immediate family, his greatest overall pain, both emotionally and physically, came from the persecution he received from his fellow Jews, particularly those who were fellow rabbis and teachers.

Wherever Paul went, he chose the Jewish synagogue as an initial platform for preaching and teaching the gospel. After his eyes were opened in Damascus, "at once he began to preach in the synagogues that Jesus is the Son of God" (Acts 9:20). When he returned to Damascus from Arabia three years later, he reentered the synagogue—only now he "baffled the Jews living in Damascus by proving that Jesus is the Christ" (9:22). And when Paul escaped from Damascus and returned to Jerusalem, we can also assume he entered the synagogues, "speaking boldly in the name of the Lord," particularly wherever he could find Grecian Jews meeting to worship. This is why his life was threatened and he had to leave after a brief ministry (9:28–30).

Local synagogues emerged during the Assyrian and Babylonian captivities and quickly became the focus of Jewish life. Any time the Jews had twelve men, they could organize a local group. In large cities like Tarsus there were a number of synagogues, just as we have a number of local churches in large cities today.

Though elders were elected to manage the affairs of each local synagogue, any competent male Israelite could read Scripture. Though such a man could also preach and explain these Scriptures, the duty of preaching and explaining was primarily an official rabbi's responsibility and privilege.

Since Paul was a renowned rabbi who had studied under Gamaliel and had served in this capacity in Tarsus for at least seven years, no one would question his right to teach in any local synagogue. Though Paul was now a Christian, he still considered himself a unique part of the Jewish community.

Consequently, when he returned to Tarsus as a believer and an apostle, he certainly would have gone to the same synagogues where he had taught years earlier as a Jewish rabbi—but now with an expanded message. He now believed with all his heart that Jesus was the Messiah promised in the Old Testament.

Paul's Personal Report

"Forty Lashes Minus One" (2 Cor. 11:24)

Many Bible interpreters believe that Paul was referring to his personal experiences in Tarsus when he outlined certain sufferings in his second letter to the Corinthians. More specifically, Paul stated that he had "received from the Jews the forty lashes minus one." Furthermore, he had received this kind of punishment a total of "five times" (2 Cor. 11:24).

This kind of flogging was a form of synagogue discipline. The apostles had already experienced this kind of punishment in Jerusalem shortly after the church was born. Members of the Sanhedrin became so jealous and angry that they "wanted to put them [the apostles] to death" (Acts 5:33). However, Gamaliel, Paul's old mentor, persuaded his colleagues not to take this kind of extreme action, the kind of murderous action they would later take toward Stephen. Consequently, they settled for "forty lashes minus one." Luke recorded that "they called the apostles in and had them flogged" and then ordered them "not to speak in the name of Jesus." They then "let them go" (5:40).

This form of punishment was rooted in the penalty for a criminal offense outlined in Deuteronomy 25:2. Forty lashes were prescribed for certain crimes. Over the years, the religious leaders incorporated this kind of flogging into their disciplinary procedures when someone violated their synagogue laws. Because of their legalism, they reduced the number of lashes to thirty-nine—just in case they miscounted. However, it was still a very cruel form of punishment that God originally designed for criminals. John Polhill describes what took place: "With bared chest and in a kneeling position, one was beaten with a tripled strap of calf hide across both chest and back, two on the back for each stripe across the chest. Men were known to have died from the ordeal."[1]

Though it's difficult to comprehend, this happened to Paul five times. Evidently he refused to stop proclaiming the message of Christ in the synagogue. Perhaps when he was excommunicated from one, he went on to another, and another, hoping his hearers would listen to his witness about the Messiah. He certainly would have shared very specifically how he had orchestrated Stephen's death and then discovered his terrible mistake when Jesus Christ appeared to him on the Damascus Road.

Some believe Paul's body was marked for life because of these beatings. There is some historical evidence Paul became "bowlegged," which "is a deformity among men who have been severely flogged."[2] Yet Paul rejoiced, like the apostles in Jerusalem, "because they had been counted worthy of suffering disgrace for the Name" (Acts 5:41; see Phil. 3:10–11). For those of us who have been free from this kind of persecution, it's difficult even to grasp this intense dedication to presenting the gospel message.

"Three Times I Was Shipwrecked" (2 Cor. 11:25)

In the same passage in Second Corinthians, Paul also referred to the fact that he "was shipwrecked" at least "three times" and "spent a night and a day in the open sea" (2 Cor. 11:25). This may have also happened during his years in Tarsus. Once he was excommunicated from the synagogues, he probably traveled along the coastline by water, disembarking in small villages where he proclaimed the gospel to the Cilician Gentiles. Supporting himself with his tentmaking skills, he carved out time to carry out the purpose for which God had called him—to go first to the Jews and then to the Greeks.

"A Thorn in My Flesh" (2 Cor. 12:7)

Paul shared another experience in his second letter to the Corinthians that happened some time during his stay in Tarsus. Describing this experience, he gave us a reference point when he stated that he knew "a man in Christ who fourteen years ago was caught up to the third heaven" (2 Cor. 12:2). It's clear from the context that Paul was definitely referring to himself (12:7–10), but it's also clear that the "fourteen years" point of reference places this experience somewhere between A.D. 41 and 43 since he wrote this letter between A.D. 55 and 57. This would put this very personal encounter with the Lord about midway during his ministry in Tarsus (see chronology chart on p. 6).

Paul described this incredible experience in very mystical terms. There were aspects about it he didn't understand himself. For example, he suspicioned that it may have been an "out-of-body" experience, but he wasn't sure. "Only God knows," he concluded (12:2–3).

Though Paul was unsure whether he was "in the body or apart from the body," he was confident that he "was caught up to paradise" and "heard inexpressible things, things that man is not permitted to tell" (12:4). "The third heaven" (12:2) or "paradise" (12:3) probably refers to the highest and most complete place where God dwells with the angels and those who have died in faith. The message Paul received was so glorious that words could not describe it, and even if he could have explained it, the Lord sealed his lips (12:4).

Because this was such a private and awesome moment in God's presence, Paul "was given . . . a thorn" in his "flesh," a messenger of Satan to torment him (12:7). But Paul never described this "thorn." We do know, however, that he prayed earnestly to have it removed. In his own words, Paul stated, "Three times I pleaded with the Lord to take it away from me" (12:8). God did not answer Paul's specific prayer but reassured him with these words: "My grace is sufficient for you, for my power is made perfect in weakness" (12:9).

We know another thing for certain about this experience. It happened in order to keep Paul from becoming prideful and arrogant. What he had seen and experienced in God's presence was such a remarkable privilege, so much so, he would not as a human being be able to keep "from becoming conceited" (12:7).

Bible scholars have speculated for centuries as to what this thorn may have been. Some believe it was physical—a bodily weakness, such as poor eyesight. Some believe it was emotional, such as a tendency to be depressed. Others believe it was spiritual—a struggle with some kind of serious temptation—perhaps sexual.

The fact is, we don't know. Obviously, the Lord doesn't want us to know or He would have told us. Perhaps He didn't want us to know so that we can relate to this experience generically. But we can certainly conclude from what we read that, in addition to persecution, Paul was eventually going to face some serious and difficult temptations. And when it happened, God promised Paul that He would give him the strength and power to endure it. Furthermore, when this incomparable power enabled him to do miraculous things, even raising the dead, he would always be aware that it was God who had enabled him to work these miracles. The ever-present "thorn" would keep him humble. Thus Paul concluded this paragraph with these words: "That is why, for Christ's sake, I delight in weaknesses, in insults, in hardships, in persecutions, in difficulties. For when I am weak, then I am strong" (2 Cor. 12:10).

Becoming God's Man Today

Principles to Live By

Principle 1. We should not be surprised when those who know us best—our family and friends— are the most resentful when we attempt to share the gospel of Jesus Christ.

If this happened to Jesus Christ and the apostle Paul, it could very well happen to us as well. Parents in particular are often the most difficult people to share with since they feel defensive. They often resent children who tell them they need a Savior because they're sinners (Rom. 3:23). Furthermore, they may feel they failed as parents, and rather than admit it may be true, they are annoyed and often become indignant.

Fortunately, this is not always true, but often it is. And when it happens, it's best to shift to a non-verbal approach to sharing the gospel and to reflect the fruit of the Holy Spirit—love, joy, peace, patience, kindness, goodness, faithfulness, gentleness, and self-control (Gal. 5:22–23).

The apostle Peter spoke to this issue quite directly in his first epistle. For those who are persecuted for doing what is right, he shared these words of wisdom:

> *But in your hearts set apart Christ as Lord. Always be pre-pared to give an answer to everyone who asks you to give the reason for the hope that you have. But do this with gentleness and respect, keeping a clear conscience, so that those who speak maliciously against your good behavior in Christ may be ashamed of their slander. (1 Peter 3:15–16)*

Principle 2. We must never take for granted the price some Christians have paid to make it possible for us to experience true freedom in Christ.

Because of the wonderful environment most of us live in—which includes the freedom to worship, to share Christ, to voice our opinions—we often assume this is the way life has always been and always will be. Not so! As we've seen, Paul suffered terribly in order to bring the gospel to his fellow Jews and the Gentiles.

Today we have thirteen letters in our New Testament that have been penned by this faithful servant of Jesus Christ. Five of these letters were actually written from prison where Paul was incarcerated because of his faithful witness. Tradition tells us that shortly after he had penned his second letter to Timothy in a Roman dungeon he became a martyr at the hands of Nero. Paul paid the ultimate price so you and I can know true freedom in Jesus Christ and have the Word of God to read and study. We must never forget that!

Over the centuries, other Christians have paid the same price as Paul. For example, William Tyndale had an insatiable passion to translate the Bible into common English so that everyone could read it. He achieved his goal to a great extent, but not without paying a terrible price. He spent seventeen months in prison and finally was burned at the stake. His dying prayer was, "Lord, open the King of England's eyes."

As a result of Tyndale's prayer and death, the rules were changed, and eventually the Scriptures *were* published in common English. In fact, the king of England eventually authorized what we have now as the King James Version of the Bible. But it took Tyndale's bold faith and sacrifice to make it happen. If we truly remember this, we will have a much greater appreciation for the Scriptures we so often take for granted. I must confess I am speaking to myself as well as to you.

Principle 3. We should continually pray for believers in various parts of the world who are enduring suffering because of their faith in Jesus Christ and their commitment to share the gospel with others.

Prayer is an amazing spiritual resource—one we don't use as we should. Though Paul was destined to suffer for Christ, he requested that the Corinthians pray for him and his fellow missionaries as they faced some frightening "hardships . . . in the province of Asia. We were under great pressure," he wrote, "far beyond our ability to endure, so that we despaired even of life." To make his point even more emphatically, he stated that they "felt the sentence of death" (2 Cor. 1:8–9).

When Paul and his companions faced this kind of persecution, he admitted that he wasn't sure of the outcome. He knew they might lose their lives, but even if they did, he knew they would be delivered—whether by "life or by death" (Phil. 1:20).

Central to Paul's enablement to face persecution with a positive attitude was the power of prayer. "On him we have set our hope," he wrote to the Corinthians, "that he will continue to deliver us as you help us by your prayers" (2 Cor. 1:10–11). Paul also reminded these Christians that "many will give thanks . . . for the gracious favor granted us in answer to the prayers of many" (1:11).

I have a close friend named Eng Go. He's Indonesian and has been a member of the church I pastor for several years. Because of our close relationship, he has shared with me some horror stories about his fellow Christians throughout the densely populated country of Indonesia. Churches have been burned, Christians have been persecuted and imprisoned, and government laws have forced many believers into poverty. Some believers have been brutally murdered.

The same could be said of countries in many other parts of the world. I've talked with pastors who were imprisoned for many years when communism dominated the former Soviet Union. In some African nations, whole groups of Christians have been shot, stabbed, and beaten to death.

Do we have a responsibility to pray for these believers even though we don't know who they are? Definitely! And prayer does change things. Though they may not be delivered from persecution, they'll find strength to face even death victoriously and experience ultimate deliverance into the very presence of the God they love and serve. We must not forget to pray for persecuted Christians.

Principle 4. We should pray continually for our government leaders so that we'll have a peaceful environment in which to live and communicate the gospel of Jesus Christ (1 Tim. 2:1–4).

In spite of the fact that many Christians have suffered over the centuries and many are suffering today, God wants us to pray for an environment free from persecution. Paul made this point clear when he wrote his first letter to Timothy. He stated:

> *I urge, then, first of all, that requests, prayers, intercession and thanksgiving be made for everyone—for kings and all those in authority, that we may live peaceful and quiet lives in all godliness and holiness. This is good, and pleases God our Savior, who wants all men to be saved and to come to a knowledge of the truth. (1 Tim. 2:1–4)*

God's plan for Paul's suffering was definitely an exception in God's scheme of things. For this we can be thankful. This passage states that it's the will of God that we *not* be persecuted so that we can live "peaceful and quiet lives in all godliness and holiness." But it's also clear why this is God's will. An environment of freedom from persecution gives all of us an opportunity to present the gospel to more people. And Paul made it very obvious that we should pray for those in authority in every culture of the world so they can continue to lead us in a way that we'll have this kind of freedom.

During the very time I did the final editing on this manuscript, I had just returned from Nigeria where I had the privilege of speaking to over four thousand African pastors. Two years earlier I had visited this same country when a ruthless dictator had ravished the entire culture. Tension, graft, and chaos had permeated the environment. But when I returned on the second trip, things were decidedly different. The dictator had died and a new man occupied the role of president—a man who had become a Christian while a political prisoner. Very quickly he was able to create a new sense of democratic freedom—not only from fear, but from persecution. The pastors I ministered to were overjoyed with this new and open environment that made it much easier for them to carry out their ministry. Their prayer for a safe, secure environment for sharing the gospel—which Paul stated we should pray for—had been answered.

Personalizing These Principles

The following questions and suggestions will help you apply the principles outlined in this chapter:

1. If your parents and Christian friends are unsaved and unresponsive to the gospel when you share it, pray that God will bring someone into their lives who will have an open door to their hearts. Above all, keep loving them as Christ loved you when you were not a believer.

2. When was the last time you stopped to think about the price some Christians have paid in order for you to be a Christian? Spend a moment thanking God for the freedom you have in Christ, and if necessary, confess the fact that you've taken this freedom for granted—at times even complaining about things that pale in view of what others have suffered so that you might know the Lord Jesus Christ as personal Savior.

3. When was the last time you prayed for Christians who are suffering in other parts of the world? What plan do you have for making this a regular part of your prayer life? Start a prayer list, beginning with the missionaries who are serving Jesus Christ in various parts of the world that are often hostile to the gospel.

4. How often do you pray for the President of the United States—regardless of his failures and sins? What about other government employees, including your state and local leaders? Add these people to your prayer list.

Set a Goal

In view of what you've learned in this study of Paul's life in Tarsus, ask the Holy Spirit to help you set one goal in order to be a more effective Christian:

_____

_____

_____

_____

Memorize the Following Scripture

*In this you greatly rejoice, though now for a little while you may
have had to suffer grief in all kinds of trials. These have come so
that your faith—of greater worth than gold, which perishes
even though refined by fire—may be proved genuine and
may result in praise, glory and honor when Jesus Christ is revealed.*
1 PETER 1:6–7

Growing Together

1. Why is it easy for Christians who live in the Western world to take their religious freedom for granted?
2. Can you share an experience in which you suffered because of your faith in Jesus Christ?
3. What kind of plan can we develop in order to pray for Christians regularly in other parts of the world who are suffering persecution?
4. Why is it easy to neglect praying for government officials?
5. What can we pray for you specifically?

Chapter 6

The Power of Prejudice

Prejudice is a horrible social disease that impacts most human beings. What makes it so difficult to deal with it in our lives—even as Christians—is that we don't recognize it for what it is. It can become a part of the fabric of our personalities and is as natural as breathing. I know. It happened to me. In fact, it took a unique crisis in my life for me to even entertain the thought that I was prejudiced.

This was definitely a problem for Jewish Christians in the first century, particularly those who lived in the vicinity of Jerusalem. Even some of God's choicest servants didn't recognize how prejudiced they really were.

A Jewish Church

During Paul's extended witnessing mission in Tarsus where he faced incredible prejudice and persecution from his fellow Jews, God was at work in the hearts of the Jewish Christians "throughout Judea, Galilee and Samaria." It was a "time of peace," as believers were "strengthened." The church "grew in numbers" as they were "encouraged by the Holy Spirit" (Acts 9:31).

But it was uniquely a *Jewish* church. Even the apostles did not believe that Gentiles could be saved—at least without first becoming converts to Judaism. This may seem strange since they were the ones who had been given the Great Commission in a special way to "go and make disciples of *all nations*" (Matt. 28:19). It was to them Jesus had said just before He ascended, "But you will receive power when the Holy Spirit comes on you; and you will be my witnesses in Jerusalem, and in all Judea and Samaria, and to the ends of the earth" (Acts 1:8).

Somehow they had missed the meaning of Jesus' words, even prior to the cross, when He identified Himself as the "good shepherd" who would lay down His "life for the sheep." Jesus went on to explain that He had "other sheep" that were "not of this sheep pen"—namely, the Gentiles. "I must bring them also," Jesus continued. "They too will listen to my voice, and there shall be one flock and one shepherd" (John 10:14–16). Clearly, Jesus was referring to the fact that He was going to die for the whole world—both Jews and Gentiles—and all were welcome into His family.

Though all of the apostles needed to personalize and internalize this great truth, the Holy Spirit zeroed in on Peter since he was the primary leader of these men. Though thousands of Jews had put their faith in Christ for salvation as a result of his preaching, he was still deluded into thinking that only Jews—and *perhaps* God-fearing Gentiles who had converted to Judaism—could be saved. What makes this even more startling is that Peter still believed this at least five years after Pentecost.

An Unsettling Vision (Acts 10:9–23)

On one occasion, Peter was in Joppa, a seaport town on the coast of the Mediterranean. He was staying with "a tanner named Simon" (Acts 9:43). One day he climbed the stairs leading to the rooftop to spend time in prayer. Down below, Simon's wife, or perhaps a maid, was preparing a meal. The aroma ascended the staircase and stimulated Peter's appetite.

The Lord used this human experience to set the stage for a supernatural revelation. Peter "fell into a trance" and had a vision (10:10). In his dream, he saw something that looked like "a large sheet being let down to earth by its four corners." It contained a variety of animals, mostly unclean as specified by Jewish law. Suddenly, Peter heard a voice, commanding him to "kill and eat."

In his dream, Peter stubbornly refused. He had never eaten unclean animals. The same thing happened two more times and again he resisted the command. Just as quickly as the sheet had appeared the first time, it disappeared. Then Peter awakened. Predictably, he was perplexed. What could this vision mean?

In God's sovereign plan, three men knocked at Simon's door just as Peter was musing over this puzzling experience. The Holy Spirit spoke directly, informing him that these men had come looking for him. "'Get up and go downstairs,'" the Spirit said. "'Do not hesitate to go with them, for I have sent them'" (10:20).

Peter, who was still confused, discovered an amazing thing as he conversed with these men. They had come from Caesarea, where they served in the household of a man named Cornelius, a wealthy Gentile. He was a centurion, a high-ranking officer in the Roman army. However, "he and all his family were devout and God-fearing" (10:2). He was also generous, helping to care for the poor, and he prayed regularly to the God of Abraham, Isaac, and Jacob.

These men explained to Peter that their master had also received a vision. He had seen "an angel of God" who informed him that the Lord had honored his prayers and his gifts to the poor. Furthermore, the angel had told Cornelius to send these men to Joppa to find Peter and to bring him back to Caesarea to meet with their master (10:3–8).

An Eye-Opening Sequel (10:23–48)

Peter understood immediately what had just happened to him on the rooftop was supernatural. It was no mere accident or normal dream. Consequently, he departed for Caesarea the next day and entered Cornelius's home. A large group had already gathered, awaiting his arrival (10:23–26).

Peter's opening comment indicates what had been the extent of his confusion regarding God's plan of salvation. "'You are well aware,'" Peter stated, "'that it is against our law for a Jew to associate with a Gentile or visit him'" (10:28). Clearly, Peter still believed the gospel was only for the Jews—at least prior to his vision in Joppa. As he began to speak, he shared his new insight—something Jesus had told him over five years before but which had not registered in his prejudiced mind and heart. "'I now realize how true it is,'" Peter admitted publicly, "'that God does not show favoritism but accepts men from every nation who fear him and do what is right'" (10:34–35).

Peter then delivered his message, a message of forgiveness through Christ's resurrection. Before he had finished, the Holy Spirit fell on these Gentiles as He had fallen on the Jewish believers on the day of Pentecost (Acts 2:1–4; 10:44–46). And just as Peter had done on that day over five years before to the Jews who had believed, he baptized these Gentile converts in Caesarea (2:41; 10:48). Another church was born—a Gentile church!

A Powerful Breakthrough (11:1–18)

When Peter returned to Jerusalem and met with the other apostles and the elders, he reiterated everything that had happened. A number of the Jewish Christians objected and criticized Peter. This couldn't and shouldn't have happened. But when they heard the whole story, much of the prejudice that had gripped their souls and blurred their objectivity began to dissipate and melt away. They actually "praised God" for what had happened (11:18).

However, their attitudes of superiority lingered. Unfortunately, it takes time to root out this kind of deep prejudice—which is evident from their positive, but still prideful response: "'So then,'" they admitted, "'God has granted *even the Gentiles* repentance unto life'" (11:18). In other words, they were saying, "It's hard to believe that God's grace could extend to people other than us, but it's true!"

A Gentile Church

The extent of Jewish prejudice among believing Jews is also very obvious in Luke's next reference in the Book of Acts. When Paul launched his persecution in Jerusalem, beginning with Stephen's death, believers left the Holy City by hordes. As we've noted, they went to Damascus, which is the reason Paul was on his way to take them into custody and return them to Jerusalem for imprisonment. But many of these people also "traveled as far as Phoenicia, Cyprus and Antioch, telling the message *only to the Jews*" (11:19).

Clearly, these persecuted Jewish Christians still believed that the message of salvation was for Jews only, not Gentiles. This should not surprise us since the apostles, their spiritual fathers and mentors, still believed the same thing.

A Ministry in Antioch

Thankfully, there was a contingency of Grecian Jews who didn't buy into this narrow view, probably because they lived among Gentiles, and did business with them and had overcome much of their prejudice. Consequently, some of those "who had been scattered by the persecution" begun by Paul (11:19)—"men from Cyprus and Cyrene, went to Antioch and began to speak to Greeks [or Gentiles] also, telling them the good news about the Lord Jesus" (11:20).

These men knew how much these pagan people needed the life-changing message of the gospel. Antioch was the third most influential city in the Roman Empire, but it was also one of the most immoral and decadent.

The Lord honored these men's efforts. The Holy Spirit convicted many people of their sins and their need for a Savior, and "a great number . . . believed and turned to the Lord" (11:21).

It took several years for this information to get back to Jerusalem. Paul had spent at least three years in Arabia, had returned to Jerusalem for a brief stay and had once again returned to Tarsus. Peter had also had his revolutionary evangelistic experience in Cornelius's home in Caesarea. When the report eventually came that many non-Jews had received Christ in Antioch, the leaders in Jerusalem were now ready to accept the possibility that "even Gentiles" could be saved. Consequently, "they sent Barnabas to Antioch" to assist these new believers (11:22).

"Son of Encouragement"

Since Barnabas was a Grecian Jew, he evidently accepted this assignment without hesitation—even with anticipation. Being "a Levite from Cyprus" (4:36), he had rubbed shoulders with Gentiles most of his life. He understood their cultural mentality. Consequently, the apostles must have reached a quick decision to send Barnabas. It's feasible he even volunteered. We must remember that the apostles had changed his name from Joseph to Barnabas, which means "Son of Encouragement," because of his sincere interest in people as well as his generous spirit (4:37).

When Barnabas arrived in Antioch, he "saw the evidence of the grace of God" in the lives of these Gentile converts (11:23), just as he had seen this "evidence" in Paul's life several years before when he had intervened for him at Jerusalem (9:26–28). Once again, Barnabas responded with trust and excitement. We read that "he was glad and encouraged them all to remain true to the Lord with all their hearts" (11:23).

Only people who are free from prejudice exhibit this kind of emotional reaction when they associate with people different from them. Barnabas saw these Gentile converts as human beings who needed a Savior and who could be transformed into the image of Christ. He realized that it was only God's grace that had saved him from eternal separation from God. Though he was a Jew, he understood why God had chosen him: not to demonstrate favoritism but to use his talents and abilities to reveal the Messiah to the whole world.

Luke has given us another reason Barnabas was able to get so excited about what God was doing among these people. "He was a good man," a righteous, God-fearing man who lived out what he believed. Furthermore, he was "full of the Holy Spirit and faith" (11:24). God had gifted him uniquely to preach the Word of God. As a result, "a great number of people were brought to the Lord."

Barnabas and Paul

We're not told how long Barnabas ministered in Antioch before he realized he needed help. It must have been a couple of years. But when the work became overwhelming, he remembered his encounter in Jerusalem with Paul, the man who claimed to be called to be an apostle to the Gentiles. He also remembered how the brothers in Jerusalem had taken him to Caesarea and then sent him off to Tarsus. Consequently, he must have gathered his leadership team in Antioch and informed them he was going to Tarsus to look for Paul in order to convince him to come to Antioch to join him in this exciting and challenging ministry.

It must have taken Barnabas some time to find Paul once he arrived in Tarsus. The little phrase "when he found him" (11:26) indicates a period of searching. This makes sense since Paul had been severely rejected by the Jews in Tarsus and may have been traveling up and down the seacoast ministering to Gentiles.

A Wonderful Reunion

Whatever the circumstances, when Barnabas found him, Paul did not hesitate to join his friend in Antioch. In fact, Paul must have been overwhelmed to meet once again the man who had been so gracious in accepting his testimony in Jerusalem and in opening the door to the apostles—to Peter particularly. You can imagine what a glorious reunion this was. It had been at least seven years since they had seen each other. Imagine the "catching-up" they had to do. And one of the most encouraging aspects of this reunion for Paul was to discover what had happened to Peter and how he had overcome his prejudice against Gentiles. Hearing about Cornelius's conversion must have also pumped new life into his heart and soul.

A Team Ministry

When Paul returned to Antioch with Barnabas, he entered into this ministry with enthusiasm (see chronology chart on p. 6). How exciting it must have been to work together with another man who shared his burden and encouraged him in his calling to be an apostle to the Gentiles. After all, Paul had evidently carried the burden in Tarsus virtually alone. But no more. Luke recorded, "For a whole year Barnabas and Saul [Paul] met with the church and taught great numbers of people" (11:26).

These Gentile "disciples were called Christians first at Antioch" (11:26). This was not necessarily an endearing term. Evidently, it was the unbelieving crowd that tagged them with this title. It may well have been used with sarcasm and a condemning attitude. But one thing is sure. They were named after the One they had committed to follow. They were not known as "Barnabasites" or "Paulites." They were followers of the Lord Jesus Christ.

A Prophetic Message and Ministry in Jerusalem

At some point during this productive era of ministry, "some prophets came down from Jerusalem to Antioch" (11:27). They were men who by the inspiration of the Holy Spirit could predict the future. Agabus was one of these gifted men. During a special gathering of the church, he "predicted that a severe famine would spread over the entire Roman world" (11:28).

The believers in Antioch responded with concern knowing that the Christians in Judea and particularly in Jerusalem would be the first to feel the negative fallout from this famine. They had long since been cut off from the welfare system in Judaism. Consequently, each Christian "according to his ability" gave to meet this need (9:29). As in all the other churches, a variety of economic levels existed. Those who could give a lot, gave a lot. Those who could not give as much, gave what they could. However, *everyone* was involved in some way.

Since this was such a significant responsibility, the church in Antioch asked Barnabas and Paul to deliver this gift of money. You can imagine what happened when they arrived on the scene. In some respects, it had to be a humbling experience for the Jewish Christians in Jerusalem who had been so hesitant to accept the fact that Gentiles could be saved. Now they were receiving gifts from these people to help them in a time of need.

A Perspective on God's Sovereign Work

Stop for a moment and review what has happened. God, in His sovereign plan, had prepared both Peter and Paul for this moment. Although the tensions between believing Jews and Gentiles were not yet formally resolved as they would be following the first missionary journey, God's plan for reaching the whole world with the gospel was on schedule. The walls of prejudice were being cracked and would eventually come crashing down. God had worked in Peter's heart through the conversion of Cornelius. His subsequent report to the elders and apostles in Jerusalem had opened the door even further. Their willingness to send Barnabas to minister to the church in Antioch confirms their new perspective on the fact that the gospel was for all people—not just for the Jews. And now that this Gentile church had sent financial help to meet the needs of believers in Jerusalem—such an act certainly verified the reality of God's grace that was at work in the pagan world. Nothing breaks down the walls of prejudice more forcefully than this kind of generosity.

Becoming God's Man Today

Principles to Live By

Principle 1. Prejudice is a subtle social disease that affects most people in the world; unfortunately, becoming a Christian doesn't automatically eliminate it from our lives.

When I first met Tony Evans at Dallas Theological Seminary in the early 1970s, I was a full-time professor and he was a student in my class where we were discussing biblical principles of church renewal. Tony was one of the few black men who were pursuing a seminary education in those days—particularly in an evangelical school.

As a result of this class and the research I was doing with my students on the theme of the New Testament church, I eventually started the first Fellowship Bible Church in 1972 and became a full-time pastor. One day Tony shared his own vision with me to start a renewal church in the black community and asked if our church (the original Fellowship Bible Church) would help finance this venture. Since we were already committed to church planting, our elders were excited about the possibility. We agreed to support Tony and his family for several years, paying their full-time salary so they could start this new church. Today that church has become the world-renowned Oak Cliff Bible Fellowship with its related ministries through the Urban Alternative.

One day, however, Tony shared with me a startling and disturbing story. Prior to attending our church, he and his family had visited a well-known evangelical church in Dallas, Texas. Following the service he and his wife were approached by a church officer and in no uncertain terms were told they were not welcome. The reason, of course, was obvious. They were black. To add insult to injury, this couple discovered that the same mentality (and carnality) existed in other Bible-believing churches that they tried to attend.

Much of this prejudicial attitude (not in every church situation) has disappeared in the Christian community, not only in Dallas, but in other parts of the United States. However, the most disturbing part of the story is that these people who attended these churches claimed to believe what the Bible teaches. Sadly, they were steeped in prejudice and were woefully violating the Word of God.

As disturbing as this story is—and it could be multiplied many times in the early seventies—it should not surprise us that this happened. Peter and the apostles believed the Word of God, but they were terribly prejudiced. Imagine being used by God to launch the worldwide church and yet believing that only Jews, or converts to Judaism, could be saved. Even being converted did not immediately root out the sin of prejudice.

Unfortunately, these attitudes still exist in pockets of people in the United States, not only in the Christian community but in the secular world as well. And we need not travel far outside the United States to discover that prejudice exists in every part of the world—in the Middle East, in Ireland, in South Africa, in China, in Russia, in short, everywhere people live. Though the message of Christianity is breaking down the walls, we must constantly remind ourselves of Paul's words to the Galatians: "There is neither Jew nor Greek, slave nor free, male nor female, for you are all one in Christ Jesus" (Gal. 3:28).

Based on these biblical words, we could expand Paul's intent to include people from all cultures of the world. When we are in Christ, there is neither black nor white, red nor yellow, rich nor poor, Swede nor Norwegian, German nor Jew, CEO nor clerk, or husband nor wife. We are Christians—which means we are one body in Jesus Christ and members of one another (Rom. 12:4–5).

Principle 2. Prejudice is rooted in sin and should be confessed to God in order to receive forgiveness.

James, the half brother of Jesus Christ and a man who served as the lead elder and pastor in the Jerusalem church, had to deal with this problem in his own life and in the Jewish Christian community. Writing to the twelve tribes (Christian Jews) who were "scattered among the nations" (James 1:1), he wrote:

> *If you really keep the royal law found in Scripture, "Love your neighbor as yourself," you are doing right. But if you show favoritism, you sin and are convicted by the law as lawbreakers. For whoever keeps the whole law and yet stumbles at just one point is guilty of breaking all of it. (James 2:8–10)*

We must call prejudice what it is. It's falling short of God's perfect standard, and that is sin. In this sense, the great apostle Peter, for at least five years after Pentecost, was living in sin when he refused to associate with Gentiles. Fortunately, God still used him to carry out His purposes in the world, but He could not use him fully until he dealt with this unrighteous attitude.

Principle 3. Prejudice can be overcome through conversion to Christ and the indwelling power of the Holy Spirit. However, in most instances, it's a process involving "the renewing of our minds."

Prejudice is like most sins. It is rooted in our minds—the way we think and feel. The key to overcoming temptation and resisting sin is to practice Paul's injunctions in his letter to the Romans. We must "not conform any longer to the pattern of this world, but be transformed by the renewing of our minds" (Rom. 12:2). When we are prejudiced, we are acting worldly. However, when we think about those things that are true, noble, right, pure, lovely, and admirable, we will renew our minds and be able to walk in the perfect will of God (Phil. 4:8).

Later in this same letter, Paul exhorted the Roman Christians—and believers of all time—to "accept one another." We are to follow Christ's example in the way He accepted us—without conditions (Rom. 15:7). All people, regardless of their race, creeds, ethnic backgrounds, economic status, and educational opportunities are welcome in the family of God. All God asks is an act of faith—believing that Jesus Christ is the Son of God and Savior of the world (John 3:16).

It always surprises people, and amazes them, when I share that I grew up in a religious community where some people believed that Jesus actually spoke German. For these people, Luther's German translation was the original Bible. Obviously, they were ignorant and did not understand that the Old Testament was originally written in Hebrew and the New Testament in Greek.

Some of these people also believed that our religious community had a special place in God's heart. We were the chosen ones. We, in essence, were better than other people. In this sense, our mentality was similar to the apostle Peter's before his encounter with Cornelius.

As I reflect on the way God dealt with this root of prejudice in my own life, I remember it took approximately five years for me even to recognize that I was plagued with this social disease. In this sense, I have something in common with Peter.

But I can also identify with Peter's desire to be a man of God—even before he recognized his prejudice. I, too, wanted to do God's will. I just didn't realize how much these prejudiced attitudes had become a part of the fabric of my personality. Consequently, God allowed me to face a crisis of faith to enable me to see my sinful condition.

I remember this painful experience well. I had just graduated from Moody Bible Institute and had moved to Billings, Montana, where I continued my education but also became involved in a ministry of music. My primary responsibility was to sing in a radio quartet on a program that aired daily.

While there, I met three key Christian leaders: a pastor, a minister of music, and a returned missionary. I became very close to all three of these men. In fact, I looked up to them as models and mentors (something I desperately needed), but eventually serious tensions developed among all three. In retrospect, I now see more clearly the reasons: misunderstandings, jealousy, hurt feelings, and of course, reactions that were more carnal than spiritual. In retrospect, I now see that God was using this experience to deal with the sin of prejudice in my own life.

At the time, I was caught in the middle. All three began to share privately what was wrong with the others. Having gone through the painful experience of leaving a religious community in order to be a part of this new religious community, I was thrown into a terrible state of disillusionment and depression. However, it was during these dark months in my life that I eventually began to see that there were serious elements of prejudice in my life that still had never been rooted out. In reality, down deep I still believed that I was better than other people. Such a belief is the essence of prejudice. This is what I had been taught all those years.

Though it took time, I eventually concluded that God was honoring my desire to be a mature Christian and allowing me to go through this period of disillusionment that eventually opened my eyes to the innermost thoughts of my heart. It was a terribly painful experience. At times, I was so depressed, I wasn't sure I wanted to live. But I needed this crisis in order for God to use me to minister to all people with a sense of humility and deep concern. I began to see that prejudice and pride are twin sins and when we deal with one, we have to deal with the other.

Personalizing These Principles

Spend time reflecting on your own attitudes and actions as a Christian. Ask the Holy Spirit to reveal any lingering prejudice in your heart and life. The following questions will help you:

1. To what extent do you believe or feel you are better than other people? Why may this be true?

2. How do you feel and act when you associate with people different from you? Are you comfortable or do you sense a feeling of superiority?
3. How do you act and feel when you are physically touched by people who are different from you? Generally speaking, do you feel comfortable or do you withdraw?

Set a Goal

Using the principles outlined in this chapter as well as the questions just outlined, ask the Holy Spirit to help you isolate your most significant need, and then set up a personal goal:

_____

_____

_____

_____

Memorize the Following Scripture

Accept one another, then, just as Christ
accepted you, in order to bring praise to God.
ROMANS 15:7

Growing Together

1. Why is it often difficult even to recognize prejudice in our lives?
2. Once we recognize personal prejudice, why is it difficult to admit it and deal with it?
3. How have you dealt with prejudice in your own life?
4. How can we best help other Christians deal with prejudice?
5. What can we pray for you specifically?

Chapter 7

A Unique Destiny

*I*n the award-winning film *Chariots of Fire,* Eric Liddell is portrayed having a heart-to-heart conversation with his sister, Jenny. They were both born of missionary parents in China, and Jenny was concerned that Eric's love for running was side-tracking him from his ministry. "I've decided I'm going back to China," he told her one day as they strolled across the gently rolling countryside. Jenny made no effort to hide her enthusiasm. She was overjoyed! "But," Eric added, "I've got a lot of running to do first."

His sister was visibly disheartened with what she heard. Her excitement level dropped immediately. "Jenny," Eric continued, sensing her disappointment, "you've got to understand. I believe God made me for a purpose, for China. But He also made me fast. I'm going to run for His pleasure."

Eric Liddell sensed he had a destiny—to serve God as a missionary in China and also to be a witness as a world-class athlete. "Run in God's name," one of his mentors had told him, "and let the world stand back and wonder." Eric Liddell went on to win in the Olympic games. "It's not just for fun," he stated. "To win is to honor Him."

Paul was also driven by his own sense of destiny. It took time for this great apostle to understand this destiny, even after his conversion on the road to Damascus. But by the time he began his missionary tours, he understood it perfectly. He knew he had an irrevocable, divine mission from God, and in many respects, a unique and special calling.

All of us as Christians are called to be witnesses for Jesus Christ in the world. We are to "shine like stars in the universe" as we "hold out the word of life" (Phil. 2:15–16). But Paul's destiny was very specific, which he described clearly in his letter to the Galatians. Returning from his first journey throughout this vast region, he wrote, "I was advancing in Judaism beyond many Jews of my own age and was extremely zealous for the traditions of my fathers. But when God, who set me apart from birth and called me by his grace, was pleased to reveal his Son in me so that I might preach him among the Gentiles. . . ." (Gal. 1:14–16).

Paul's Divine and Detailed Preparation

God began to prepare the apostle Paul for ministry as a missionary even before he was born, and this preparation continued prior to his "new birth." We've looked at his preconversion years, but let's review these experiences with a new perspective—the specific way God was preparing him to carry out his destiny, even before he became a Christian (To understand more clearly the way God prepared Paul for his primary ministry as a church planting missionary, see the chronology chart on p. 6 as you read the following review.)

Preconversion Preparation

Paul was born into a very dedicated and committed Jewish family. For the first thirteen years of his life, he learned the Old Testament from his father's knee in his hometown of Tarsus. To further his religious education, his parents then sent him to Jerusalem where he studied for at least six years under the great rabbi Gamaliel. There he learned all the detailed laws of Pharisaical Judaism.

Following this Jewish education that was second to none, he returned to Tarsus as a devoted rabbi in his own right. There he continued his education in Greek and Roman philosophy. Little did he realize how he would draw upon his secular education once he became a Christian.

When Paul returned to Jerusalem to persecute Christians, he was approaching thirty-three years of age and was well-grounded in his Jewish faith as well as secular thought—far more so than any others his own age. Little did he realize that God would soon build upon this foundation to make him one of the greatest Christian evangelists and apologists of all time.

Post-Conversion Preparation

Following Paul's conversion on the road to Damascus, he spent at least three years in Arabia. God was continuing to prepare him to carry out his calling. During this time, he probably went through a period of deprogramming. It was more than a time of unlearning and relearning. He began to integrate what he had learned about Old Testament truth and secular thought with New Testament truth—something he had never heard before.

At the end of three years, Paul came back to Damascus and began a ministry among his fellow Jews. However, this period of time was brief because he was not yet prepared to carry out the purpose for which God had called him. Paul was forced out of Damascus because of persecution and then decided to go to Jerusalem to meet the apostle Peter.

It was during this visit in Jerusalem that Paul first met Barnabas who introduced him to the apostles. He could stay only for a brief period of time in the Holy City; and then went back to his hometown, the city of Tarsus. However, this time he returned as a Christian.

Paul ministered in Tarsus for approximately seven years, but, probably unknown to him, this time was still ministry preparation. In fact, it was a very intense learning experience. As we've seen, he suffered a great deal of persecution.

While there, Paul was in for a wonderful surprise. One day Barnabas, who had been ministering to Gentiles in Antioch of Syria, came looking for him. They hadn't seen each other since Paul had left Jerusalem for Tarsus. When the work in Antioch had become overwhelming to Barnabas, he remembered this Jew-turned-Christian whom he had met in Jerusalem and introduced to the apostles. He also remembered that Paul believed he had a special calling to reach Gentiles with the gospel.

Paul wasted no time joining Barnabas in Antioch. Luke recorded, "So for a whole year Barnabas and Saul met with the church and taught great numbers of people. The disciples were called Christians first at Antioch" (Acts 11:26).

It was in Antioch, working alongside Barnabas, that Paul took his final step in ministry preparation. Barnabas became his special tutor. The Lord was using this intern experience to prepare him for his great missionary task: to carry the gospel to the Gentile world.

Paul's Divine and Direct Calling

Approximately eleven or twelve years after he was converted to Christ, Paul was now ready for his first missionary trip. In many respects, this calling to begin this ministry was as direct as his Damascus Road experience when Jesus Christ called him to be a Christian. This time, however, the Holy Spirit spoke directly to several men who were identified as "prophets and teachers" (13:1). We read that "Barnabas, Simeon called Niger, Lucius of Cyrene, Manaen (who had been brought up with Herod the tetrarch) and Saul" were together "worshiping the Lord and fasting" (13:1–2). It was then that the Holy Spirit spoke directly to these five men and delivered a very specific and direct message: "Set apart for me Barnabas and Saul for the work to which I have called them" (13:2).

These were not psychological impressions. God had spoken with specific words and His message was crystal clear. Paul was now ready for a very intense ministry to the Gentiles approximately forty-five years after he had been born.

At this point, we can assume these five men called the whole church together and explained in detail what had happened. In the presence of all of these believers in Antioch, Simeon, Lucius, and Manaen "placed their hands on" Barnabas and Paul "and sent them off" (13:3).

Paul's Divine and Determined Mission

Just as Paul's detailed preparation and direct calling were divine, so was his determined mission. The Holy Spirit had called them and the same Holy Spirit had sent them on their way. It was definitely a "determined mission" for Paul because it involved incredible dedication and commitment to carry out the destiny to which God had called him. F. F. Bruce states that Paul was a "man of vision" and a "man of action."[1]

Paul's First Missionary Journey at a Glance (See Figure 2)

- Arrived in Salamis on the island of Cyprus, which was Barnabas's homeland. (13:4; 4:36)

- Preached in the Jewish synagogues. (13:5)

- Traveled through Cyprus and arrived at Paphos, the seat of the Roman government; Sergius Paulus, a man who served as a Roman governor in Cyprus, converted to Christ. (13:6–12)

- Left Cyprus and sailed to Perga in Pamphylia; here John Mark left Barnabas and Paul and returned to Jerusalem. (13:13)

- Leaving Perga (at sea level), traveled 100 miles inland to Antioch in Pisidia (an elevation of 3,600 feet); emerging as team leader, Paul delivered a lengthy apologetic message in

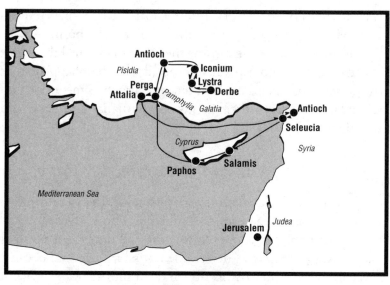

Figure 2
Paul's First Missionary Journey

the synagogue; both Jews and Gentiles responded to the gospel, causing intense jealousy among the non-responding Jews; hereafter Luke referred to "Paul and Barnabas" rather than to "Barnabas and Paul." (13:14–52)

- Traveled east to Iconium; again began preaching in the Jewish synagogue; "spent considerable time there" but were forced to leave the city because of Jewish opposition. (14:1–7)

- Traveled to Lystra, a totally Gentile and pagan city; Paul and Barnabas worshiped as gods because Paul had healed a crippled man; Paul later stoned because Jews from Antioch and Iconium came and turned the people against the apostles. (14:8–20)

- Paul miraculously healed from his injuries; went on to Derbe; many responded to the gospel. (14:21a)

- Returned to Lystra, Iconium, and Antioch to minister to the new Christians; appointed elders in every church. (14:21b–23)

- Returned to Perga to preach. (14:24–25a)

- Traveled to Attalia. (14:25b)

- Returned to Antioch in Syria, where they reported on their missionary activities and "stayed there a long time with the disciples." (14:26–28)

Important Observations

1. Paul quickly emerged as the primary leader of this mission-ary team (Acts 13:2, 7, 13). Paul began his team ministry in Antioch as an associate to Barnabas. This is clear from the "name order" in Luke's account. We read that for a whole year "Barnabas and Saul [Paul] met with the church" (11:26). At the end of this year, when these two men were called and commissioned to begin their first extended missionary tour, the Holy Spirit again made it clear who was to be the leader of the team: "The Holy Spirit said, 'Set apart for me Barnabas and Saul [Paul] for the work to which I have called them'" (13:2).

However, this was soon to change. By the time this missionary team left the island of Cyprus, Paul was definitely in charge. We read that it was "Paul and his companions" who boarded ship and "sailed to Perga in Pamphylia" (13:13).

2. Paul's new leadership role was confirmed by a supernatural event (Acts 13:6–12). Something very important happened on the island of Cyprus that caused this transition and shift in leadership. Though Sergius Paulus, the proconsul or Roman governor on the island, had asked to have an audience with "Barnabas and Saul [Paul]"—indicating he knew who was leading this team—it was Paul who stepped forward and performed a very dramatic miracle. A sorcerer named Elymas, sensing that Sergius Paulus was interested in the gospel message, tried to interfere (13:8). Having received a direct revelation from the Lord, Paul boldly stepped forward and confronted Elymas with a blunt message, calling him "a child of the devil and an enemy of everything that is right!" (13:10). Paul, endued with God's power, struck this evil man with blindness.

As far as we know, this was the first time the Holy Spirit enabled Paul to perform this kind of dramatic miracle, verifying that he was indeed a true apostle. Paul later wrote about this verification in his second letter to the Corinthians. Speaking of his own ministry, he wrote: "The things that mark an apostle—signs, wonders and miracles—were done among you with great perseverance" (2 Cor. 12:12).

In this instance, on the island of Cyprus, the Holy Spirit enabled Paul to look right into this sorcerer's innermost being and read his mind. Paul next pronounced God's judgment on Elymus, striking him blind. And at this moment, this supernatural event became a watershed experience for both Paul and Barnabas—which leads to our next observation.

3. Barnabas recognized Paul's divine calling as an apostle and willingly took a secondary and supportive role. From the first time Barnabas met Paul in Jerusalem, heard his testimony, and then built a bridge for him to the other apostles, he knew this man had a special calling to minister to the Gentiles. It explains why he went to Tarsus and brought Paul back to minister in the Gentile church in Antioch. However, what happened on the island of Cyprus convinced Barnabas it was time to step aside and allow Paul to fulfill his special apostolic calling. He now saw his friend in the same role as Peter, James, and John—and the others whom Jesus Christ called to be His apostles (Matt. 10:1–4; Mark 3:13–19; Luke 6:12–16). Consequently, Barnabas willingly reversed roles, no doubt initiating the shift. What a tribute to the reason Barnabas had been selected by the apostles in Jerusalem to minister to Gentile converts in Antioch: "He was a good man, full of the Holy Spirit and faith" (Acts 11:24). He did not allow ego and pride to cause him to hold on to his primary leadership role.

4. Paul's special calling became obvious in the city of Antioch (13:44–52). When "Paul and his companions" disembarked at Perga in Pamphylia, they began one of the most difficult aspects of the journey as they made their way to Antioch in Pisidia. In some places, the narrow road cut straight up the mountain. This was a "secondary Roman road" that was not designed for chariots and carts. Wild tribesmen attacked lone travelers, making it necessary for people to travel in caravans. During the day, the sun's heat was so stifling that they had to break camp before sunrise and stop at noon. Each night they had to build a huge fire to keep warm. And the next morning when they broke camp, they hoped to make at least fifteen miles of the one hundred-mile trek that lay ahead.

When Paul, Barnabas and young John Mark landed in Perga and inquired about this journey over this treacherous mountain terrain, we can assume they received a number of warnings about this dangerous journey. It's not surprising that at this point young John Mark bailed out and returned to Jerusalem—something Paul had difficulty accepting and forgetting (Acts 15:37–38). In the early days of his ministry, he had very little tolerance for people who weren't willing to pay the same price he paid in order to carry out the Great Commission.

When Paul and Barnabas arrived in Pisidian Antioch after a difficult and arduous journey, they discovered a strong contingency of fellow Jews. They waited for the Sabbath and then visited the local synagogue. After the usual "reading from the Law and the Prophets," the synagogue rulers—who recognized these men as Jews—invited Paul and Barnabas to share "a message of encouragement" (13:15).

There is no question who was the new leader. Paul stood up immediately and spoke with knowledge and authority, drawing upon everything he had learned from his parents and his old mentor, Gamaliel. He reviewed Israel's history from their ancient fathers to the time of King David. But Paul also shared what he had learned and believed about the death and resurrection of Jesus Christ.

Paul spoke with such power that word spread throughout the whole region. In fact, on the very next Sabbath day—after Paul and Barnabas had been invited to speak again—Luke recorded that "almost the whole city gathered to hear the word of the Lord" (13:44).

Predictably, the Jews who did not respond to the gospel became insanely jealous—demonstrating a pattern that would be repeated again and again. As Paul looked out at these men and women, he looked into faces filled with rage—a reflection of his own emotional reactions when he had authorized Stephen's death. It was then that he turned to the Gentiles in Pisidian Antioch, sharing the good news that Jesus Christ had died for the whole world.

Once again, the Holy Spirit affirmed his unique calling. Many responded to the gospel (13:48). But the Jewish hostility escalated, and eventually Paul and Barnabas had to leave this region and travel on to Iconium, but not until Paul's apostolic calling to minister to Gentiles was once again verified. They left a growing and thriving church (13:52).

5. Paul (and Barnabas) passed the true ministry test in Lystra (Acts 14:8–20). When this missionary team arrived in Iconium, they experienced a repeat performance on the part of both Jews and Gentiles. Many received the gospel message and believed in Jesus Christ. But many rejected it and tried "to mistreat them and stone them" (14:5). But God once again protected these men and they traveled on to Lystra, where they faced one of their greatest challenges.

When they arrived, which seemed to be an even more pagan city than Antioch and Iconium, Paul noticed a man who had been lame from birth. As Paul was sharing the good news regarding Jesus Christ, he noticed that this man was listening very intently. Sensing that "he had faith to be healed," Paul performed another marvelous miracle (14:9–10), not anticipating what was about to happen. The pagan people in Lystra concluded that the Greek gods, Zeus and Hermes, had become incarnated as human beings. They thought Barnabas was Zeus and Paul was Hermes "because he was the chief speaker" (14:12).

Paul and Barnabas were mortified and chagrined. Rejecting the people's efforts to offer sacrifices to them, they tried to explain they were just men representing "the living God, who made heaven and earth and sea and everything in them" (14:15).

But during this incredible scene, some influential Jews "came from Antioch and Iconium and won the crowd over" (14:19). In their fickleness, the very people who wanted to worship Paul and Barnabas as Greek gods turned against them. Targeting Paul—which demonstrates again his prominence as a leader of the team—they literally dragged him outside the city and stoned him, leaving him for dead. What an incredible reflection of what Paul had done to Stephen years before!

But Paul's days on earth were not over. He was just beginning his ministry to the Gentile world. Miraculously, God enabled him to recover from what everyone believed was a state of death. Luke recorded that "he got up and went back into the city," and "the next day he and Barnabas left for Derbe" (14:20). Again the Lord was verifying Paul's apostolic calling.

6. Paul was committed to carrying out both directives in the Great Commission (Matt. 28:19–20). After Paul and Barnabas had a successful ministry, leading many to the Lord Jesus Christ in Derbe, "they returned to Lystra, Iconium and Antioch, strengthening the disciples and encouraging them to remain true to the faith" (Acts 14:21–22). In other words, these two men were committed not only to making disciples but to teaching them and to building them up in the faith—just as Jesus had commanded when He issued the Great Commission to the "eleven disciples" on a mountain in Galilee (Matt. 28:16–20). When Paul and Barnabas first arrived in Antioch, Iconium, and Lystra, they carried out in a special way the first part of Jesus' command—to "make disciples" by leading people to Jesus Christ. When they returned to these cities, they concentrated on the second part of Jesus' command—to teach these new believers, grounding them in their faith and preparing them to face ongoing persecution.

However, Paul and Barnabas took an additional step—something Jesus had not included in the Great Commission but had illustrated powerfully in His own ministry. Just as the Lord had equipped the apostles to continue the ministry He began, Paul and Barnabas sought out godly Christian men they could appoint as elders in each church (Acts 14:23). They knew that if their ministry was going to continue and multiply, each congregation needed qualified leaders.

It's logical to ask where these men came from. How could they become mature so quickly—mature enough to measure up to the standard Paul later outlined in his letters to Timothy and Titus. Elders were to be men who were "above reproach" (that is, men with good reputations) because they were morally pure, temperate, self-controlled, respectable, hospitable, able to teach, not given to drunkenness, not violent but gentle, not quarrelsome, not lovers of money. Where did they find men so quickly who were managing their own families in a respectable fashion (1 Tim. 3:1–7; Titus 1:6–9)?

The answer to this question is really quite simple. In every one of these cities, there were God-fearing Jews—men like Stephen and Philip who first served as deacons in the church in Jerusalem and then as evangelists. There were also men like Cornelius from Caesarea who was a God-fearing Gentile, a man of prayer and generosity, even before he became a Christian. By the time Paul and Barnabas had returned to these cities, approximately two years later, these men had grown tremendously in their faith. In fact, these God-fearing Jews and Gentiles were actually men of character before they understood and received the gospel.

Paul and Barnabas concluded this first missionary tour in approximately three years.[2] Returning to Antioch in Syria, where they had begun, "they gathered the church together and reported all that God had done through them and how he had opened the door of faith to the Gentiles" (Acts 14:27). We're not told how long they stayed in Antioch, but Luke reported that it was "a long time" (14:28).

Becoming God's Man Today

Principles to Live By

Principle 1. God wants all of us to learn from our own life experiences in order to serve God.

Paul's life and destiny were unique. This is indisputable. But in essence, all Christians have a unique calling and destiny, regardless of our backgrounds. Paul made this crystal clear when he penned these powerful and reassuring words in his letter to the Romans:

> And we know that in all things God works for the good of those who love him, who have been called according to his purpose. For those God foreknew he also predestined to be conformed to the likeness of his Son, that he might be the firstborn among many brothers. And those he predestined, he also called; those he called, he also justified; those he justified, he also glorified. (Rom. 8:28–30)

God didn't cause Paul to sin against Stephen or the other Christians he had persecuted and put to death. Neither does He cause other people to sin against Himself or others—including you and me. However, if we are true believers, God has had His hand on our lives, even before we were born. I cannot comprehend or explain this incredible reality and mystery, but I believe it is true.

God's grace in saving Paul in spite of his terrible sins motivated him to serve the Lord with all his heart until the day he died. Everywhere he went, he shared the message that he wrote to Timothy:

> Here is a trustworthy saying that deserves full acceptance: Christ Jesus came into the world to save sinners—of whom I am the worst. But for that very reason I was shown mercy so that in me, the worst of sinners, Christ Jesus might display his unlimited patience as an example for those who would believe on him and receive eternal life. (1 Tim. 1:15–16)

*Principle 2. God wants all of us to mentor others who
may become more prominent than we are.
Furthermore, we will share in their eternal rewards.*

When Paul wrote his final letter to Timothy, he exhorted him to do exactly what Barnabas had done for him: "You then, my son, be strong in the grace that is in Christ Jesus. And the things you have heard me say in the presence of many witnesses entrust to reliable men who will also be qualified to teach others" (2 Tim. 2:1–2).

One day I was sitting in the reception room waiting to see the president of Moody Bible Institute. Suddenly, I noticed a plaque on the wall that made reference to the Sunday school teacher who led D. L. Moody to Christ in the back room of a Boston shoe store. At age seventeen, this event changed this young man's life and set him free to realize the destiny God had called him to fulfill.

As I reflected on D. L. Moody's conversion and subsequent ministry, I could not help but think about the fact that very few people know the name of this Sunday school teacher. However, D. L. Moody's name and accomplishments are recorded in the history of Western civilization.

Because of this Sunday school teacher's example and impact on D. L. Moody's life, Moody started his own Sunday school in Chicago which eventually became the great Moody Church. Later, Moody became a powerful evangelist who was used by God to bring many people to Jesus Christ throughout the United States and Great Britain. Eventually, he expanded his ministry to include theological education and started a Bible institute in Chicago, which was named Moody Bible Institute after his death.

Yes, we remember D. L. Moody, but most of us know next to nothing about the man who led him to Christ and mentored him in his new faith. However, God knows who he is. Personally, I believe Edward Kimball will share in every reward D. L. Moody receives at the judgment seat of Christ—the rewards for all the people who came to Christ through his evangelistic ministry and every person who ever studied at Moody Bible Institute. In fact, because I graduated from Moody, if there are any spiritual rewards for writing this book on Paul's life, D. L. Moody's Sunday school teacher will also share in the eternal rewards.

Multiply this concept millions and millions of times. Add to my personal illustration all of the millions and millions of books that have ever been published and distributed by Moody Press. Think if you can, of all the multiplied millions of people who have been ministered to by the extensive radio ministry at Moody Bible Institute. Calculate if you can, the number of people who have come to Christ through the graduates of Moody. Statistics demonstrate that nearly ten percent of all Protestant missionaries have studied at Moody Bible Institute. Humanly speaking, it's difficult to imagine an equity system this comprehensive for every Christian who has ever lived. However, we must not forget that God is omniscient. He never forgets what His children have done to advance the kingdom. God has designed the ultimate "networking system" and never forgets anyone's contributions to His work.

We may not remember D. L. Moody's Sunday school teacher, but God does, and His great "computer system" never crashes. God will correctly calculate every reward due him. Personally, I believe Barnabas, in his own way, understood this wonderful reality when he stepped aside as Paul's mentor and became his associate. As we'll see, Barnabas's name and activities soon disappear in Luke's historical account, and Paul occupies center stage. However, this man's accomplishments did not disappear from God's eternal records. Everything that Paul ever accomplished for Jesus Christ has also been credited to Barnabas's account (Phil. 4:17).

Principle 3. All glory and honor ultimately belongs to God, not to us.

Both Paul and Barnabas illustrate this principle in a dramatic way. When the people of Lystra wanted to worship them as Greek gods, these men "tore their clothes and rushed out into the crowd, shouting: 'Men, why are you doing this? We too are only men, humans like you'" (Acts 14:14–15). They immediately pointed these people to God and His Son Jesus Christ.

Many Christians pay lip service to this example. However, their total lifestyle violates what they say. It's easy to say that we are giving all glory to God but then to live for ourselves. When we look at the way we use our time, if we're honest, we'll have to admit that we're using it for ourselves. When we look at our talents, we're using these gifts primarily to build up ourselves. When we look at our treasures—our material possessions—how much are we *really* giving to God compared with what we are keeping for ourselves?

Paul and Barnabas gave glory and honor to God and were willing to demonstrate the truthfulness of this statement no matter what the cost to them personally. What an incredible example of commitment and dedication!

Personalizing These Principles

1. To what extent do you believe Romans 8:28, even though you don't understand this great truth?

   To help you personalize this principle, make a list of the good things that have happened in your life as well as the bad things. Next to the bad things, write out a statement on how God can use these negative experiences—as bad as they were—in your own life to help others.

   To help you personalize this truth even further, meditate on Paul's words to the Corinthians: "Praise be to the God and Father of our Lord Jesus Christ, the Father of compassion and the God of all comfort, who comforts us in all our troubles, so that we can comfort those in any trouble with the comfort we ourselves have received from God" (2 Cor. 1:3–4).

2. To what extent are you mentoring others, trusting God to use them even beyond anything you might be able to accomplish?

Can you remember people whom you have mentored and discipled who are now occupying positions that are greater than your own? Have you ever been tempted to feel badly—even jealous and angry—because they are more prominent than you are?

These are human emotions. Though Barnabas may have been tempted with the same feelings, there is no evidence he ever allowed Paul's role as the leader of the team to cause him to act out these feelings in negative ways. For example, some Bible interpreters believe that John Mark may have gotten angry and returned to Jerusalem because his "Uncle Barnabas" was replaced by Paul. If this played any part in Mark's decision, there is absolutely no evidence that Barnabas had a personal problem allowing Paul to become the leader.

On the other hand, have you been mentored by someone you've forgotten? In fact, if it had not been for that person's influence in your life, you would not be doing what you are doing today.

Set a Goal

As you reflect on the principles in this chapter that emerge from both Paul's life and that of Barnabas, what changes do you need to make? Ask the Holy Spirit to enable you to set at least one goal:

_____

_____

_____

Memorize the Following Scripture

And we know that in all things God works for the good of those who love him, who have been called according to his purpose.
ROMANS 8:28

Growing Together

1. Would you share how God has enabled you to turn "lemons into lemonade" in your own life? Why is this a difficult process?

2. How do you guard against taking glory for yourself that belongs to God but at the same time accepting encouraging comments from others because of your own human effort?

3. Have you had the privilege of mentoring someone who is now exceeding your own accomplishments? How does this make you feel? Why is this sometimes a difficult experience?

4. Can you think of someone who has mentored you? How have you expressed your appreciation to this person? What can you do that you're not already doing?

5. What can we pray for you specifically?

Chapter 8

Controversy in the Christian Community

When I first became a Christian, I viewed the Bible as a "book of rules." The reason is easy to explain. That's the way I'd been taught, both in my church and in my home. I grew up believing I had to do certain things before God would accept me as His child. Once I became a Christian, there were also certain things I believed I needed to do—or not do—in order to keep myself from being eternally lost. Needless to say, my life was not a very happy existence. I did not understand the difference between law and grace.

Unexpected Crises

Paul faced this kind of confusion in the New Testament world. In fact, three rather distressing things happened after he and Barnabas returned from their first missionary journey.

- First, the key leader of the apostles—none other than Peter himself—came to Antioch and compromised the freedom we have in Christ.

- Second, Paul received a very distressing report regarding the churches that he and Barnabas had founded in the province of Galatia.

- Third, some Judaizers came to Antioch from Jerusalem and began teaching the Gentiles that they could not be saved unless they were circumcised according to the law of Moses.[1]

The Conflict in Antioch

When Paul and Barnabas arrived in Antioch, they immediately called a meeting and "reported all that God had done through them and how he had opened the door of faith to the Gentiles" (Acts 14:27). This was particularly encouraging to the Christians in Antioch since most of them were Gentiles who had also come to faith in Christ. However, in the midst of this excitement, Paul encountered some serious theological problems. The first one involved the apostle Peter—one of the most difficult assignments Paul ever had to face. Peter's behavior was inconsistent with the gospel of God's grace.

Peter's Inconsistency

When Paul wrote to the Galatians, he described Peter's inconsistent behavior and how he had to confront him. His words more than speak for themselves:

> *When Peter came to Antioch, I opposed him to his face, because he was clearly in the wrong. Before certain men came from James, he used to eat with the Gentiles. But when they arrived, he began to draw back and separate himself from the Gentiles because he was afraid of those who belonged to the circumcision group. The other Jews joined him in his hypocrisy, so that by their hypocrisy even Barnabas was led astray. (Gal. 2:11–13)*

The picture is clear. Peter, who had already been confronted by God Himself because of his prejudice against Gentiles, was doing the opposite of what he knew was the right thing to do. He understood by direct revelation it was not wrong for a Jewish Christian to eat with a Christian Gentile

(Acts 10:28). Consequently, when he came to Antioch and "saw the evidence of the grace of God," he was probably just as excited as Barnabas when he first arrived on the scene (11:23).

But then it happened. Some men came from Jerusalem. Even though they professed faith in Jesus Christ as the Messiah, they still believed it was necessary for Gentiles to become Jews before they could become Christians. More specifically, they believed these Gentiles had to be circumcised.

Because these Christian Judaizers were outspoken and strong leaders and would stir up tension in the church in Jerusalem when they returned by reporting on Peter's association with Gentiles, he chose to avoid the issue by withdrawing from these believers. A number of other Jewish Christians followed suit—including Barnabas.

Paul's Confrontation

Seeing the impact of Peter's inconsistency, even on his loyal missionary companion, Paul could not stand idly by. Peter's behavior clearly sent a message that was out of harmony "with the truth of the gospel" (Gal. 2:14). Consequently, he publicly confronted him with his hypocrisy. He then turned to the crowd of onlookers and made the message of the gospel crystal clear:

> *"We who are Jews by birth and not 'Gentile sinners' know that a man is not justified by observing the law, but by faith in Jesus Christ. So we, too, have put our faith in Christ Jesus that we may be justified by faith in Christ and not by observing the law, because by observing the law no one will be justified." (Gal. 2:15–16)*

To be sure, confronting Simon Peter was terribly difficult and traumatic for Paul. After all, Peter *was* the great apostle to the Jews, the man Jesus Christ had appointed to play a key role in launching the church. He was indeed the leader of all the other apostles. Paul must have felt a great sense of anxiety, especially in view of his own preconversion acts of violence against Christians, to now have to confront Peter with his hypocrisy. But to be true to what he believed with all his heart to be right, he had no choice.

A Distressing Report

The problem Paul faced with Peter was not an isolated incident in the New Testament world. While Judaizers were creating a problem in Antioch which led to Peter's hypocrisy, they were also infiltrating the churches Paul and Barnabas had planted in the Galatian region. This was even more disturbing to Paul since they had risked their lives when they had returned to Lystra, Iconium, and Antioch of Pisidia in order to strengthen these believers. No doubt, some of the elders they had appointed to lead these churches had also betrayed their trust (Acts 14:21–23). If it could happen to the apostle Peter, it certainly could have happened to these men who were relatively new converts.

Paul was not only disappointed in these Galatian Christians but he was also intensely angry at these false teachers for trying to lead these believers astray. His caustic words speak for themselves:

> *I am astonished that you are so quickly deserting the one who called you by the grace of Christ and are turning to a different gospel—which is really no gospel at all. Evidently some people are throwing you into confusion and are trying to pervert the gospel of Christ. But even if we or an angel from heaven should preach a gospel other than the one we preached to you, let him be eternally condemned! As we have already said, so now I say again: If anybody is preaching to you a gospel other than what you accepted, let him be eternally condemned! (Gal. 1:6–9)*

Predictably, these false teachers had also attacked Paul's credibility. Consequently, he went on to defend his apostolic calling to preach the gospel to the Gentiles (1:11–24). He also let them know that James, the primary leader in Jerusalem, as well as the apostle Peter and the apostle John had given him and Barnabas "the right hand of fellowship when they recognized the grace" God had given to Paul. "They agreed," Paul continued, "that we should go to the Gentiles, and they to the Jews" (2:8–10). It was then that Paul also shared with these Galatian Christians the experience he had had with Peter, having had to confront him face-to-face with his own hypocrisy (2:11–13).

We can only imagine the emotional pain this report caused Paul. However, the Holy Spirit used it in his life to pen a letter that has positively impacted some of the greatest Christian minds of all times—including Martin Luther and John Calvin, who both wrote commentaries explaining this epistle. These two reformers underscored the very same truth again and again that drove Paul to write this letter in the first place— that all people, both Jews and Gentiles, are justified by faith in Christ and not by observing the law (Gal. 2:16).

Judaizers from Judea

To add insult to injury, Luke has recorded that a group of men "came down from Judea to Antioch" and taught "the brothers: 'Unless you are circumcised, according to the custom taught by Moses, you cannot be saved'" (Acts 15:1). This disconcerting challenge evidently came on the heels of Paul's disagreement with Peter as well as the distressing report that had come regarding the Galatian churches. No sooner had he penned this letter to these Christians, emphasizing that "in Christ Jesus neither circumcision nor uncircumcision has any value" and that "the only thing that counts is faith expressing itself through love" (Gal. 5:6), he faced a circumcision controversy in his own home church.

These men from Jerusalem were adamant in what they believed. Consequently, Paul and Barnabas faced another challenging confrontation. What must have been even more distressing is that they could not resolve the problem through public debate. Try as they might, tension continued to build, so much so that what happened in Antioch is described by Luke as a "sharp dispute." Tempers flared and the open controversy deteriorated into heated arguments and dissention. These "Judaizers from Judea" simply wouldn't back down.

The Jerusalem Council

At their wit's end, the leaders in Antioch appointed Paul and Barnabas and some other respected Christians in the church "to go up to Jerusalem to see the apostles and elders" and to seek their help in resolving this circumcision controversy (15:2). When they arrived, they were warmly welcomed and Paul and Barnabas "reported everything God had done through them" (15:4). Luke's dramatic account of what happened speaks for itself:

Persistent Resistance

> Then some of the believers who belonged to the party of the Pharisees stood up and said, "The Gentiles must be circumcised and required to obey the law of Moses." (Acts 15:5)

Peter's Affirming Message

> "Brothers, you know that some time ago God made a choice among you that the Gentiles might hear from my lips the message of the gospel and believe. God, who knows the heart, showed that he accepted them by giving the Holy Spirit to them, just as he did to us. He made no distinction between us and them, for he purified their hearts by faith. Now then, why do you try to test God by putting on the necks of the disciples a yoke that neither we nor our fathers have been able to bear? No! We believe it is through the grace of our Lord Jesus that we are saved, just as they are." (Acts 15:6–11)

Another Report by Barnabas and Paul

The whole assembly became silent as they listened to Barnabas
and Paul telling about the miraculous signs and wonders God had
done among the Gentiles through them. (Acts 15:12)

James's Positive Response

"Brothers, listen to me. Simon has described to us how God at
first showed his concern by taking from the Gentiles a people for
himself. The words of the prophets are in agreement with this, as it
is written:

> *'After this I will return*
> > *and rebuild David's fallen tent.*
> *Its ruins I will rebuild,*
> > *and I will restore it,*
> *that the remnant of men may seek the Lord,*
> > *and all the Gentiles who bear my name,*
> *says the Lord, who does these things'*
> > *that have been known for ages.*

It is my judgment, therefore, that we should not make it dif-
ficult for the Gentiles who are turning to God. Instead we should
write to them, telling them to abstain from food polluted by idols,
from sexual immorality, from the meat of strangled animals and
from blood. For Moses has been preached in every city from the
earliest times and is read in the synagogues on every Sabbath."
(Acts 15:13–21)

A Watershed Experience

What happened in Jerusalem is an important event in
church history. I've called it a "watershed experience" since the
decisions that resulted clarified in the minds of believing Jews
and Gentiles that salvation is by grace through faith and not by
the works of the law. Had this not happened, we might have
witnessed major splits in the churches that had been planted in
the Gentile world. Paul's instructions and exhortations in the

Galatian letter would have been undermined and rejected by Jewish Christians. On the other hand, the letter would have been accepted by many Gentile Christians and the split between both Jew and Gentile believers would have been widened—perhaps never to be mended. However, the decisions to accommodate without compromising the pure message of the gospel set the stage for Paul's continued ministry, both in his missionary preaching and through the twelve other epistles that he wrote.

Peter's Mature Response

It's obvious from Peter's positive report that Paul's confrontation in Antioch had hit home. He was now on the same team. What makes this so significant is that Peter does not appear to be intimidated by the elders and the other apostles. He was leading with strength and confidence. His message was clear, and there doesn't seem to be any evidence of lingering prejudice. He now understood true freedom in Jesus Christ— the message Paul explained so clearly in his letter to the Galatians (Gal. 5:1, 13).

James's New Perspective

We also see dramatic changes in James, the Lord's half-brother and the senior elder in the church in Jerusalem. His eyes were now open. He could interpret the Old Testament prophets without reading into their thoughts his own prejudiced thinking. Peter's previous experience with Cornelius had also impacted James's theology. It seems that his speech was the message God used to bring a final resolution to the law-and-grace controversy.

The Specific Solution (Acts 15:22–29)

The apostles and elders in Jerusalem agreed with both Peter and James. Consequently, they penned a letter to the Gentile believers in Antioch, Syria, and Cilicia and chose Judas and Silas, two of their most trusted leaders, to deliver the epistle to these churches. Brief and to the point, the letter stated: "It seemed good to the Holy Spirit and to us not to burden you with anything beyond the following requirements: You are to abstain from food sacrificed to idols, from blood, from the meat of strangled animals and from sexual immorality. You will do well to avoid these things" (Acts 15:28–29).

It may appear that this letter was compromising the doctrine of grace by requiring certain things for salvation. Not so. Note again James's statement. He made it clear that what he was sharing was his "judgment"—his opinion (15:19). He was concerned that they not make it difficult for Gentiles to come to Christ by requiring Jewish traditions. On the other hand, he was also concerned that they should not make it difficult for Jews to come to Christ by attacking *their* customs—particularly regarding eating meat that was sacrificed to idols, drinking blood, and eating meat of strangled animals.

This is why he said, "'For Moses has been preached in every city from the earliest times and is read in the synagogues on every Sabbath'" (15:21).

Regarding abstaining from sexual immorality, this certainly was a requirement for godly living for both Jews and Gentiles, although it was certainly not a requirement for salvation. However, it was one of the first signs of a true conversion experience in being "imitators of God." Paul made this clear again and again in his letters to these new believers. For example, when he wrote to the Ephesian Christians, he said, "But among you there must not be even a hint of sexual immorality, or of any kind of impurity, or of greed, because these are improper for God's holy people" (Eph. 5:3).

The Resolution (15:30–35)

Judas and Silas delivered this powerful little letter to the Christians in Antioch. Not surprisingly, the response was very positive. The believers were encouraged—probably as much with the unity that had been restored as with the message itself. These men eventually returned to Jerusalem, and Paul and Barnabas continued to have a fruitful ministry in Antioch—which set the stage for the second missionary journey.

Becoming God's Man Today

Principles to Live By

The principles that flow from these difficult and dramatic confrontations form the bedrock of Christian theology. Though this was a very difficult period in church history, without these guidelines, Christianity would have deteriorated into just another religion based on religiosity, "churchianity," and so-called good works.

Principle 1. Salvation is a free gift from God that is received by faith and is made secure by God's eternal power.

Peter made this point crystal clear when he addressed the apostles and elders in Jerusalem. "'We believe,'" he said without equivocation, "'it is through the grace of our Lord Jesus that we are saved'" (Acts 15:11). In other words, it's not the things we do or don't do that give us eternal life. In fact, some of the most moral people in the world are lost because they have not put their faith in Jesus Christ to save them. No amount of good works can make us righteous before God.

Years later, when Paul wrote to the Romans, he underscored this great truth. "We have been justified through faith" and because we are, he continued, "we have peace with God through our Lord Jesus Christ, through whom we have gained access by faith into this grace in which we now stand" (Rom. 5:1–2).

Furthermore, once we are saved, we are secure because of God's power—not our own efforts. Once we put our faith in Jesus Christ and are redeemed, we are "marked in him with a seal, the promised Holy Spirit, who is a deposit guaranteeing our inheritance until the redemption of those who are God's possession" (Eph. 1:13–14). It is God's power that has saved us, and it's God's power that keeps us saved. When this great truth penetrated my own heart, it changed my life as a Christian.

But you say, what about the way we live? What about good works? This is a very appropriate question, which leads to our next principle.

Principle 2. Godly works will characterize our lives if we are truly saved.

Holy living is a sign of our salvation. For example, after Paul wrote to the Ephesians and told them that they had been saved by grace through faith apart from works, he proceeded to tell them that as Christians "we are God's workmanship, created in Christ Jesus *to do good works*, which God prepared in advance for us to do" (Eph. 2:10, emphasis added). In other words, if we are truly saved, good works will eventually follow.

James also spoke to this issue. "Faith by itself," he wrote, "if it is not accompanied by action, is dead" (James 2:17). In other words, it's possible to claim to have faith yet to have a faith that is "dead." It is a mere profession; we are still living in darkness.

This does not mean that the moment people believe in Jesus Christ and are born again that they will automatically live godly lives. They must be taught the will of God, especially if they're converted out of a pagan lifestyle that reflects a non-biblical value system. This is also why Jesus said, "Therefore go and make disciples . . . teaching them to obey everything I have commanded you" (Matt. 28:19–20).

The Corinthian Christians are a classic example. Before they became Christians, many of them were "sexually immoral . . . idolaters . . . adulterers . . . male prostitutes . . . homosexual offenders . . . thieves . . . greedy . . . drunkards . . . slanderers" and "swindlers" (1 Cor. 6:9–10). Paul concluded this list by saying, "And that is what some of you were. But you were washed, you were sanctified, you were justified in the name of the Lord Jesus Christ and by the Spirit of our God" (6:11).

When Paul left these Christians to continue on his missionary journey, he later wrote a letter and addressed the sinful behavior that continued to exist in the church. Though he addressed them as people who were "sanctified in Christ Jesus and called to be holy" (1:2), he went on to indict them for living "worldly" lives. They were still "mere infants in Christ" (3:1). In fact, if it were not for the supernatural gifts of the Spirit they had received when they believed, he wouldn't have recognized that they were Christians. They were acting like "mere men" (3:4).

The Corinthians were definitely "carnal" or "worldly" Christians—a concept some people try to deny. But to eliminate this category is to deny that the Corinthians were Christians and to ignore the numerous references in Paul's letter to their position in Christ (1 Cor. 1:2, 5, 8, 10, 26, 30; 3:1, 9, 16; 4:15; 6:2, 5, 11; 12:27; 15:1–2, 58).

The important point to note is that Paul addressed their sins specifically as being out of the will of God—their divisiveness (3:3–4), their arrogance and pride (4:18), their immorality (5:1), their disputes before pagan judges (6:1–2), their lack of concern for weaker brothers and sisters (8:11–13). He also addressed their gluttony, drunkenness, and selfishness at the Lord's table (11:20–22). But when Paul confronted them, they began to change and to conform their lives to Jesus Christ. This happened because they were true Christians, people converted out of degenerate paganism. Had they rejected Paul's exhortations, they would have been demonstrating that they were "illegitimate children and not true sons" (Heb. 12:8). This happened because true believers "are God's workmanship, created in Christ Jesus to do good works, which God prepared in advance for us to do" (Eph. 2:10). In other words, if we are truly saved by grace through faith, good works will eventually follow.

Principle 3. Our Christian lives should not be characterized by either legalism or by license.

It's human nature to go to extremes in almost every arena of life—whether in politics, economics, philosophy, psychology, education, or religion. Unfortunately, this also happens in biblical Christianity. Some believers are bound up in legalism—a rule-book approach to life. Others go to the other extreme and promote and practice license—that once we're saved by grace, there are no specific do's and don'ts.

Becoming Acceptable to God

I was reared in a legalistic environment. I was taught that if I wanted to be accepted by God, I needed to do several things—go through a period of remorse, confess my sins to one of our church elders, attempt to make right everything I had ever done wrong, go before the congregation to be questioned about my spiritual experience (called "proving"), be baptized by immersion, and then receive the Holy Spirit when the leaders in the church laid their hands on me. Once I had completed all of these things, I was received into membership and *hopefully*, would enter heaven some day—*if* I continued to be obedient to the rules of the church.

As I studied my New Testament, I began to see that these requirements were not in harmony with the biblical message. Paul's references to Abraham's salvation experience impacted me in a special way. Even before Christ came, this Old Testament patriarch was saved by faith and faith alone—when he "'believed God and it was credited to him as righteousness'" (Rom. 4:3). But Paul went on to point out that Abraham was saved—"made righteous"—*before* he was circumcised. This Old Testament rite became "a seal of the righteousness that he had by faith while he was still uncircumcised" (4:10–11).

Just so, Paul explained, Abraham is the "father of all who believe" (4:11). We too are saved by faith and faith alone. To make this point crystal clear, Paul elaborated:

> *The words "it was credited to him" were written not for him alone, but also for us, to whom God will credit righteousness—for us who believe in him who raised Jesus our Lord from the dead. He was delivered over to death for our sins and was raised to life for our justification. Therefore, since we have been justified through faith, we*

have peace with God through our Lord Jesus Christ, through whom
we have gained access by faith into this grace in which we now stand.
And we rejoice in the hope of the glory of God. (4:23–5:2)

I'll never forget the first time this great truth penetrated my mind and heart. After struggling for several years with the assurance of my salvation, I was meditating one day on this section of Paul's letter to the Romans. Joy and peace flooded my soul when I realized that I was saved by grace through faith—and not by works.

Don't misunderstand. This doesn't mean we should not be baptized. Jesus commanded that those who follow Jesus Christ should have this experience (Matt. 28:19), and we see this illustrated again and again in the Book of Acts (Acts 2:41; 8:13, 38–39; 9:18–19, 16:15, 33; 18:8). But like circumcision in the Old Testament, baptism is a symbol of what has already happened between us and God. By faith, we die with Christ and are resurrected to a new life. In fact, from God's point of view, when we believe and pass from death to life, "God raised us up with Christ and seated us with him in the heavenly realms in Christ Jesus" (Eph. 2:6). Water baptism simply bears witness to this wonderful reality.

Continuing to Be Acceptable to God

Inseparably related to a legalistic view of salvation is that we keep ourselves saved—hopefully—by what we do or do not do. For me, it meant obeying all the rules of the church. One of those rules was not to attend any religious meetings other than those in my own church or other churches in our own particular denomination. To be honest, I began doubting this doctrine even before I joined this religious group. However, because of the fear that had been generated because of my belief system, I felt very guilty and insecure when I violated this "rule." Even though I knew in my head there were true believers outside of my religious community and I had the freedom to fellowship with them, my heart was filled with tension.

I remember so well when my younger brother and I would secretly slip away from our community and attend Youth for Christ meetings at Winona Lake, Indiana. Because we didn't have enough money for a motel, we slept in my dad's car. Though I was excited about the meetings and highly motivated to share my faith with others, I always returned experiencing a lot of fear and anxiety. I was afraid of being found out and confronted by the leaders in the church.

A second by-product of this kind of theology caused me to evaluate my eternal relationship with God by how I felt at any given moment. Because I was struggling internally with contradictory messages, I often felt sad and depressed. Unfortunately, during these times, I doubted my salvation simply because I didn't "feel" saved.

For me, understanding "justification by faith" was like a "second conversion." It changed my life and set me free to serve Christ without fear. I knew nothing would "be able to separate" me "from the love of God that is in Christ Jesus our Lord" (Rom. 8:31–39).

But you say, doesn't this lead to license—living any way we want to live? After Paul had expounded this great truth in Romans—that we are justified by faith and faith alone—he faced the same question head-on. "What shall we say, then?" he asked. "Shall we go on sinning so that grace may increase?" Paul answered his own question emphatically: "By no means! We died to sin; how can we live in it any longer?" (6:1–2).

In the Introduction to this study, I shared a wonderful and additional life-changing experience when I began to understand that God's grace not only provides for our salvation but teaches us to live godly lives. Nothing could be clearer in Paul's letter to Titus. The following words eliminate both legalism and license:

> *For the grace of God that brings salvation has appeared to all men. It teaches us to say "No" to ungodliness and worldly passions, and to live self-controlled, upright and godly lives in this present*

age, while we wait for the blessed hope—the glorious appearing of
our great God and Savior, Jesus Christ, who gave himself for us to
redeem us from all wickedness and to purify for himself a people
that are his very own, eager to do what is good. (Titus 2:11–14)

Personalizing These Principles

Evaluate your own Christian experience in view of the events described in this chapter as well as the biblical principles that emerge from the way Paul interacted with these events. The following questions will help you make this biblical truth a part of your life:

1. To what extent do you understand and believe that your salvation is a free gift from God—something you cannot and did not work for?

2. To what extent do you have the assurance of your salvation and that God is the one who keeps you eternally saved? In other words, to what extent do you understand that your eternal redemption is not dependent upon your own efforts?

3. When you evaluate your Christian lifestyle, what evidence do you see that you are truly saved?

4. When you look at how you live your Christian life, what evidence is there of legalism—either in your view of how you were saved or what keeps you saved? On the other hand, what evidence is there of license—that is, living your life in such a way that you are taking advantage of God's grace?

Set a Goal

In light of the way you have answered the above questions, what one goal do you believe the Holy Spirit wants you to set for your life right now?

_____

_____

_____

_____

_____

Memorize the Following Scripture

For the grace of God that brings salvation has appeared to all men. It teaches us to say "No" to ungodliness and worldly passions, and to live self-controlled, upright and godly lives in this present age, while we wait for the blessed hope—the glorious appearing of our great God and Savior, Jesus Christ, who gave himself for us to redeem us from all wickedness and to purify for himself a people that are his very own, eager to do what is good.
TITUS 2:11–14

Growing Together

1. Why do so many people have difficulty believing that salvation is a free gift apart from works of any kind?
2. When you became a Christian, what was the first indication that you were a true believer?
3. How has God disciplined you when you have deliberately violated His will?
4. What are some of the evidences that you've seen in Christians that indicate they are being legalistic? On the other hand, what evidences are there that they are guilty of license—that is, taking advantage of God's grace?
5. What can we pray for you specifically?

Chapter 9

Forgetting What Is Behind and Pressing On

Watching Christian leaders fail can be a very disillusioning experience—especially if it is a serious moral and ethical issue. I've seen both, and it's always difficult to handle emotionally and spiritually. But there are also some human mistakes that can be encouraging, especially when the leader is a strong Christian. And of course, no matter how spiritual we are as leaders, we all fail. In fact, one of the reasons we can trust the revealed Word of God is the way biblical authors have exposed the weaknesses and foibles of some of the most godly leaders, both in the Old and the New Testaments.

This is certainly true of Luke's recording of Paul's life and ministry in the Book of Acts. He could have conveniently omitted the next paragraph in this dynamic, historical account just to make Paul look good (Acts 15:36–41). After all, he was the great apostle to the Gentiles. His calling was clearly super-natural, involving a person-to-person encounter with Jesus Christ after the Lord had returned to heaven. Luke could have easily rationalized, reasoning that to let the whole world know about Paul's attitudes and actions at this moment in his life would hurt the Christian movement. Not so!

To me, this event in Paul's life made him an even greater hero. His well-known and immense strengths are less intimi-dating when I see some of his weaknesses. It's encouraging to discover that God used him even though he wasn't perfect. Furthermore, and more importantly, he was willing to change.

Devoted Brothers

Paul and Barnabas had exemplified trust, loyalty, mutual support, and oneness in heart and mind. Remember the first time Paul returned to Jerusalem? It was Barnabas who reached out to him when the other Jerusalem Christians didn't trust him (9:26–27). Later, when Barnabas needed an associate pastor in Antioch, he sought out Paul in Tarsus and asked him to assist in this great and challenging work (11:25–26). And when the church in Antioch needed men to deliver a gift of money to help with the famine relief in Judea, they chose these two men, knowing they were a trustworthy team that had demonstrated a spirit of one-mindedness during the year they had ministered in this great church (11:30).

The greatest demonstration of their friendship, however, happened on the first missionary journey. Shortly after this tour began, Barnabas willingly and humbly moved over as the leader of the team and encouraged Paul to take the reigns and exercise his apostolic role. Together, they faced persecution in nearly every city, never allowing pressure and self-interests to divide them. And when they returned after nearly three years of grueling ministry, they both shared what God had done among the Gentiles, never attempting to upstage each other (14:27).

Another wonderful illustration of their commitment to one another came when they faced the circumcision controversy. They stood side-by-side before the apostles and elders in Jerusalem and defended salvation by grace through faith. In fact, Paul actually stepped aside from his lead role on this missionary team and encouraged Barnabas to be the spokesman, knowing his companion had more credibility among these Jewish believers (15:12). He had not forgotten that it was the Christians in Jerusalem who had placed their trust in Barnabas and sent him to Antioch to give oversight to this Gentile church (11:22). Whatever temptation Paul may have had at that moment to demonstrate his divine call before his Jewish brothers in Christ, he did not yield. God's kingdom work was far more important to Paul than trying to prove to the apostles and elders in Jerusalem that he was the leader of this missionary team.

As a result of the Jerusalem council meetings, a letter was written "to the Gentile believers in Antioch, Syria, and Cilicia," resolving the law-grace issue. Paul and Barnabas then returned to Antioch and continued their ministry for a period of time, teaching and preaching "the word of the Lord" (15:35). Again, there is absolutely no sign of tension between them. Though Paul had become the leader, they served together, not only as fellow missionaries and brothers in Christ, but as great friends.

An Unexpected Argument

Against the backdrop of this incredible and exemplary team unity, it's rather jolting to see Paul and Barnabas face what to them was an irreconcilable disagreement. Their tempers flared, and they separated and went different ways. Luke minced no words in reporting this incident.

How It Happened

The tension began when Paul proposed that they "'go back and visit the brothers in all the towns where'" they had "'preached the word of the Lord'" (15:36). They had left many of these Christians to face persecution because of their faith in Jesus Christ. Paul knew many had also been led away from the gospel of grace and had been taught that they needed to become Jews before they could become Christians. Furthermore, he was probably wondering how the Galatians had responded to his straightforward letter and at times caustic words when he addressed the false teachers and those who had become confused.

Barnabas was also genuinely concerned and initially thought Paul's suggestion was a great idea. However, he was adamant about taking John Mark with them. Although this young man—Barnabas's cousin—had bailed out early on during the first journey and returned to Jerusalem (13:13), he wanted to give him another chance. Barnabas had certainly spent time talking with John Mark when he and Paul attended the council meeting in Jerusalem. In fact, Paul and Barnabas may have stayed in Mark's home. We can imagine the tearful conversation as this young man poured out his sadness and disappointment in himself for having "deserted" the missionary team "in Pamphylia" (15:38). Barnabas certainly would have sympathized with his remorse and would have done all he could to give him a second chance.

At this juncture, it would be easy to accuse Barnabas of nepotism since Mark was his relative. However, there is no evidence this was the case. In this instance, we see the same concern Barnabas had demonstrated toward Paul on a previous occasion when he had been rejected by Christians in Jerusalem (9:26–27). In like manner, he wanted to give his cousin an opportunity to redeem himself. Barnabas was so loyal to the misjudged that he was willing to risk his relationship with others to right a wrong—in this case, his best friend and fellow missionary.

A "Sharp Disagreement"

Paul disagreed with Barnabas, and Luke has made it very clear why he felt this way. Mark had not hung in there when things got tough. Paul was obviously disappointed in Mark. He had lost trust in this young man—and perhaps some respect. He feared that he would do the same thing on the second journey. After all, Paul knew they would face the same kind of difficult circumstances, perhaps even worse. He was also well aware that persecution and suffering were going to be an ongoing part of his ministry, wherever he went, among both Jews and Gentiles. The Lord had made this very clear in

Damascus following his conversion (9:16). To Paul, common sense dictated this would not be a wise decision.

Barnabas refused to give in and Paul became even more adamant about his own position. They both bristled and exchanged some very heated words. In fact, "they had such a sharp disagreement," Luke wrote "that they parted company" (15:39). More literally, these two giants in the faith became very irritated with each other because neither would concede. Consequently, Barnabas took Mark and "sailed from Cyprus" and Paul decided to invite Silas to join him on the second journey—one of the two men chosen by the church in Jerusalem to deliver the letter to the Gentile believers (Acts 15:22).

Mark's Restoration

We are not told specifically what happened to Barnabas and John Mark when they left Paul in Antioch and arrived in Cyprus. However, we can be certain they continued their ministry together. But we can also be sure that Paul and Mark were reconciled.

Ministry in Prison

Years later, Mark visited Paul and ministered to him during his first imprisonment in Rome. Consequently, we read in Paul's letter to the Colossians, "My fellow prisoner Aristarchus sends you his greetings, as does Mark, the cousin of Barnabas" (Col. 4:10). And then, Paul implied that he had sent these believers previous instructions about Mark, briefing them on his commitment to Jesus Christ and the gospel. We read, "If he [John Mark] comes to you, welcome him."

During his second imprisonment, this time in a Roman dungeon, Paul wrote his second letter to Timothy. Once again he mentioned John Mark in even more enduring terms. Knowing his time was short before he would be sentenced to death by the wicked and unpredictable Nero, he wrote: "Get

Mark and bring him with you, because he is helpful to me in my ministry" (2 Tim. 4:11).

This final reference to Mark in this last letter Paul ever wrote leaves no questions as to Paul's renewed relationship with the young man he had once rejected. Whatever trust was missing was restored. Whatever disappointment Paul experienced had dissipated.

Peter's Associate

Tradition also tells us that John Mark also became an associate to the apostle Peter, a logical assumption in view of their relationship in Jerusalem. This dynamic apostle had often spent time in Mark's home, where the church met frequently for worship and teaching (Acts 12:12–14) and in his first epistle, he identified him as "my son Mark" (1 Pet. 5:13).

Mark's Gospel

Even though details are sparse regarding Mark's ministry after he joined Barnabas, one thing is certain. This young man who was intimidated by persecution and who may have chafed under the wear and tear of traveling over treacherous Roman roads and into hostile cities was eventually given an honor received by very few. Though he had been rejected at one point in time by the apostle Paul, the Holy Spirit chose him to record the life of Christ—which today we call the Gospel of Mark.

Who Was Right and Who Was Wrong?

This is a difficult question. Any answer is speculative, but I have my own opinion.

Loyalty to People

I have great respect for Barnabas, who was willing to stand firm for what he believed was an unfair and insensitive decision on Paul's part. It took a lot of courage and internal fortitude.

Barnabas knew Paul was called by the Lord Jesus Christ personally to be the great apostle to the Gentiles. He knew how devoted he was to preaching the gospel, regardless of intense persecution. He also knew how committed he was to communicating the truth. But more importantly, Paul was his close friend. In spite of all these factors, in this instance Barnabas believed Paul was wrong, primarily because he was being insensitive to a young man who had no doubt admitted his failure and wanted a second chance.

Devoted to the Gospel

On the other hand, Paul's devotion to Jesus Christ and the gospel has been unequaled throughout church history. It's difficult to conclude that this devoted Christian leader who had done so much for all of us could have made a mistake when he refused to give John Mark a second chance. But, from a human point of view, I believe he did. At this moment in his life, his greatest strength may have become his greatest weakness. His commitment to be uncompromising in preaching the pure gospel of God's grace may have spilled over into his Christian relationships. He was so unswerving in his desire to preach the good news that he forgot that this "good news" is what transforms our lives and affects the way we treat people.

We must also remember that this determination flowed naturally out of Paul's basic personality that led him in his non-Christian life to launch a terrible persecution against the church, beginning with the approval of Stephen's death. When he became a Christian, he was just as zealous for the truth of the gospel as he was for what he believed was the "truth" of pharisaical Judaism. Carrying out every jot and tittle of the law sometimes overshadowed the way he impacted people.

"As Iron Sharpens Iron"

We can only speculate regarding Paul's future relationship with Barnabas. However, it's inconceivable they failed to be reconciled. They were both godly men with deep spiritual convictions. In fact, I personally believe they crossed paths again, embraced and glowingly reminisced regarding their dynamic ministry together prior to their disagreement.

There is a proverb that reads: "As iron sharpens iron, so one man sharpens another" (Prov. 27:17).

This is certainly what happened to Paul and Barnabas. They had been too loyal to each other to allow any negative feelings to continue to harm their relationship in Christ. Furthermore, they both believed and taught relational reconciliation and forgiveness. Not to practice these biblical exhortations would contradict their deepest spiritual values.

We must always remember, too, that Paul was a human being who needed to grow in his Christian experience just as any other person. And what makes him an even greater model is that he did just that. This becomes increasingly clear as we look at his expanded Gentile mission.

Paul's Second Journey

At first glance, it appears that Paul and Silas left Antioch together. However, both Silas and Judas, the men commissioned by the apostles and elders to deliver the letter they had composed to the Gentile churches, had returned to Jerusalem prior to this serious disagreement between Paul and Barnabas (15:33). Consequently, Paul evidently ventured out on this second journey alone, "commended by the brothers to the grace of the Lord" (15:40). Luke then recorded that "he [Paul] went through Syria and Cilicia, strengthening the churches" (15:41).[1]

Back Home Again

Paul certainly would have stopped in Tarsus, his home city, where he had ministered for at least seven years before joining Barnabas in Antioch. What a rewarding experience it must have been for him to discover that many of his converts were still following Jesus Christ, especially since he had faced incredible persecution during this period of time. It would have been a grand reunion as he embraced these believers and encouraged them to continue growing in their faith.

Face-to-Face Communication

From Tarsus, Paul entered the Galatian region (see fig. 3). He arrived first in Derbe, where he and Barnabas had "preached the good news" and had "won a large number of disciples" (14:21). On this second visit, Paul concentrated on establishing these believers in the faith.

By this time, they would have received and read Paul's "Galatian letter," which would have given these believers an opportunity to respond to some of the very straightforward things Paul had written. After all, he had called them "foolish" for allowing false teachers to lead them astray (Gal. 3:1). This could easily be interpreted as being brash and insensitive—especially by new believers. All of us tend to remember this kind of communication, especially when it is written rather

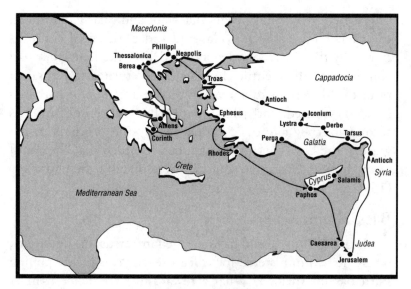

Figure 3
Paul's Second Missionary Journey

than shared face-to-face. Consequently, Paul may have had to "mend some emotional fences" before he could build deep relationships with these people.

In addition, Paul certainly had to confront some of the false teachers who would still be attempting to convince these Gentile believers that they needed to become Jews and keep the Law of Moses before they could be saved. This would have been a very difficult task, especially since Paul had to face these Judaizers alone. But he never retreated from this kind of confrontation. He never "hesitated to proclaim . . . the whole will of God" (Acts 20:27). This was one of his greatest strengths—though some would have criticized him for being mean-spirited.

A New Team

When Paul left Derbe, he returned to Lystra (16:1)—just as he and Barnabas had done on their first journey (14:21)—which made this his third visit to this city (compare fig. 2, p. 110 with fig. 3, p. 148).

Another Partner

This was an emotionally rewarding experience for Paul. As far as we can tell, Silas arrived, coming directly from Jerusalem after he had gotten word that Paul had invited him to be his partner on the second journey.

What a reunion this must have been. During the first leg of this journey, Paul would certainly have spent many sleepless nights reflecting on his dispute with Barnabas. Traveling alone would have intensified his ambivalence about what had happened. After all, he and Barnabas had preached together in these same cities and had suffered serious and painful persecution.

You can imagine what a balm this was to Paul's heart and spirit when Silas arrived. It also gave him a unique moment to share his loneliness since leaving Antioch and how much he must have missed Barnabas. It would also have given him a needed opportunity to talk things through regarding his feelings of regret about what had happened—feelings he must have had even if he still believed he was right. Silas certainly would have offered a sympathetic and listening ear.

A Second Chance

Something else happened in Lystra that, in some respects, gave Paul an opportunity to "undo what he had done." He met a young man named Timothy, who had probably become a Christian on Paul's first visit to Lystra. In fact, Timothy probably watched in emotional horror and torment as he saw Paul stoned and left for dead. In all probability, he was one of "the disciples" who "had gathered around" Paul as he lay bleeding and wounded "outside the city." But imagine Timothy's amazement when this dynamite apostle began to stir and miraculously "got up and went back into the city" (14:19–20). If he hadn't witnessed this awesome event firsthand, he certainly heard about it immediately.

Timothy continued to grow in his Christian faith during Paul's absence. The other Christians in his own city and even in neighboring Iconium took note of him. Consequently, when Paul arrived in Lystra on the second journey, Luke has recorded that "the brothers in Lystra and Iconium spoke well" of him (16:2). Paul was very impressed with what he heard and even more impressed with what he saw and invited this young man to join his missionary team.

Unique Changes

Timothy was a product of a "mixed marriage." His "mother was a Jewess and a believer," and his "father was a Greek" (16:1). As a result, he had never been circumcised. What may be a surprise move in view of Paul's strong statements in his Galatian letter about the spiritual meaninglessness of circumcision (Gal. 5:1–6), he nevertheless had Timothy circumcised. Luke tells us why. It was "because of the Jews who lived in that area, for they all knew that his father was a Greek" (Acts 16:3).

"All Things to All Men"

How can we explain this? First, it demonstrates that Paul was developing more wisdom and cultural sensitivity in his own approach to preaching the gospel. There are things that definitely cannot be changed without compromising the pure message of the Word of God. But there are some things that are really not important when it comes to the true message of hope in Christ—such as circumcision or uncircumcision. In fact, Paul later made this point very clear in his letter to the Corinthians—a church that was founded on this second journey. He wrote:

> *Though I am free and belong to no man, I make myself a slave to everyone, to win as many as possible. To the Jews I became like a Jew, to win the Jews. To those under the law I became like one under the law (though I myself am not under the law), so as to win those under the law. To those not having the law I became like one not having the law (though I am not free from God's law but am under Christ's law), so as to win those not having the law. To the weak I became weak, to win the weak. I have become all things to all men so that by all possible means I might save some. I do all this for the sake of the gospel, that I may share in its blessings. (1 Cor. 9:19–23)*

Don't misunderstand. Paul never compromised the fact that we are "saved by grace through faith" and never by works of any kind. If anyone thought that circumcision was necessary for salvation, Paul would quickly have rejected this kind of message. But knowing how important "circumcision" was to dedicated Jews, he encouraged Timothy to be circumcised so they would have a more open door to these people in preaching the gospel of God's grace. His real concern was "circumcision of the heart, by the Spirit, not by the written code" (Rom. 2:29). Paul changed his method but never his message.

The Thessalonian Example

There was something else transpiring in Paul's heart and life following his conflict with Barnabas over John Mark. He began to realize that the way we treat people is a very important part of our Christian witness. This can be illustrated by what happened in Thessalonica.

After Paul and Silas left Lystra and crossed over the Aegean Sea as a result of a vision from a "man in Macedonia" (Acts 16:6–10), they eventually came to Thessalonica (see fig. 3). Again they faced intense persecution, but they didn't leave until a number of people believed in the Lord Jesus Christ (Acts 17:4). However, Paul was deeply concerned about these new believers and how they would respond to persecution. Would they grow in their faith or turn back to their pagan ways? Consequently, when this missionary team arrived in Athens, Paul sent Timothy back to Thessalonica, not only to see how these new Christians were doing, but to encourage them in their faith (1 Thess. 3:1–2).

Timothy brought back a glowing report (3:6). The Thessalonian believers were "standing firm in the Lord" (3:8). Paul wanted to return and help them even more, but since he couldn't, he wrote them a letter known as First Thessalonians. As he encouraged them to continue to mature in their faith, Paul gave us a unique glimpse into the spiritual and emotional growth that had taken place in his own life and ministry.

First, he illustrated his ministry among them with a beautiful and intimate metaphor: "But we proved to be gentle among you, as a nursing mother tenderly cares for her own children" (1 Thess. 2:7, NASB).

Second, he illustrated this same ministry by referring to the way a father should relate to his own children. Again, note the following: "You are witnesses, and so is God, of how holy, righteous and blameless we were among you who believed. For you know that we dealt with each of you as a father deals with his own children, encouraging, comforting and urging you to live lives worthy of God, who calls you into his kingdom and glory" (1 Thess. 2:10–12).

This does seem to be the same Paul we encountered in his early ministry. He had grown in his ability and capacity to relate to people with gentleness and tenderness. He had matured in his own Christian life and this is what makes him one of the greatest Christians who ever lived. Though called by Jesus Christ Himself to be the great Apostle to the Gentiles, he practiced what he preached to the Ephesians and to all of us—"to put off your old self" and "to be made new in the attitude of your minds; and to put on the new self, created to be like God in true righteousness and holiness" (Eph. 4:22–24).

The Barnabas Influence

Paul and his missionary team went on to complete this journey and eventually returned to Antioch in Syria (see fig. 3). But there is one other very significant change in his life. We can see this in the way he encouraged Timothy in spite of this young man's areas of vulnerability. Like John Mark, Timothy could be easily intimidated. Paul understood this from the very day they left Lystra. Consequently, he initially protected Timothy from some of the most difficult aspects of the ministry. He allowed him to work behind the scenes—otherwise, he, too, would have been "stripped and beaten" and "thrown into prison" when they were in Philippi. However, only Paul and Silas "were severely flogged" and then incarcerated (Acts 16:22–24).

As you follow their ministry career together, it appears that Paul did not want Timothy to become so discouraged that he would give up and return to his home in Lystra. He gave Timothy time to grow and mature, something he failed to do with John Mark. This is beautifully illustrated in the way he sent him back to Thessalonica to check on the church. After a number of serious but sheltered encounters with the enemies of the cross, Paul knew that Timothy was now ready for this challenging task. But he never pushed Timothy beyond his capabilities. And when he got discouraged and intimidated, he took time to encourage him with positive feedback. This is very clear in Paul's second letter to Timothy. Listen to Paul's words which he wrote from a Roman prison:

> *I thank God, whom I serve, as my forefathers did, with a clear conscience, as night and day I constantly remember you in my prayers. Recalling your tears, I long to see you, so that I may be filled with joy. I have been reminded of your sincere faith, which first lived in your grandmother Lois and in your mother Eunice and, I am persuaded, now lives in you also. For this reason I remind you to fan into flame the gift of God, which is in you through the laying on of my hands. For God did not give us a spirit of timidity, but a spirit of power, of love and of self-discipline. So do not be ashamed to testify about our Lord, or ashamed of me his prisoner. But join with me in suffering for the gospel, by the power of God. (2 Tim. 1:3–8)*

Becoming God's Man Today

Principles to Live By

Paul's experience as a maturing Christian is a great example. Following are some very specific principles that are certainly applicable to our lives today.

Principle 1. No matter what our status and position as Christians, we need to continue to become more and more like Jesus Christ, not only in what we believe doctrinally, but in the way we live out what we believe in our relationship with others.

Early on in his ministry, Paul focused more on doctrine and truth. However, the more he matured in his relationship with Jesus Christ, the more he matured in his relationship with others—both Christians and non-Christians. He understood more fully what John meant when he described Jesus as being "full of grace and truth" (John 1:14).

During his first imprisonment in Rome, he bore witness to his own spiritual journey. He had been a dynamic Christian for nearly thirty years, yet he wrote:

> *Not that I have already obtained all this, or have already been made perfect, but I press on to take hold of that for which Christ Jesus took hold of me. Brothers, I do not consider myself yet to have taken hold of it. But one thing I do: Forgetting what is behind and straining toward what is ahead, I press on toward the goal to win the prize for which God has called me heavenward in Christ Jesus. All of us who are mature should take such a view of things. (Phil. 3:12–15a)*

What did Paul forget? Did he not remember his murderous activities toward believers when he tried to stamp out Christianity? Did he not remember his insensitivity toward John Mark and his harsh words in his letter to the Galatians? Of course not. What Paul "forgot" was his tendency—one we can all identify with—to concentrate on his failures and mistakes. Paul understood that Christ's blood continues to "purify us from all unrighteousness" (1 John 1:9). His lifetime goal was to become more like Christ and not to allow the sins of the past to inhibit his forward progress. This is God's will for all Christians.

After having taught young people at both the Bible college and seminary level for nearly twenty years, I became involved in church planting—which I've now done for over twenty-five years. My first church was an overnight phenomenon, growing by leaps and bounds. From the mother church, we planted five daughter churches in the first five years.

It was during this very successful period of ministry that I made one of my biggest mistakes—to appoint men to eldership who were immature. In some ways, Paul's weakness (to be insensitive and over-demanding) was my strength—to trust young men. However, this strength also became my greatest weakness and it created some severe problems, not only for several of the churches we planted but for these young leaders themselves. Some were not ready for the positions I assigned them, and they failed.

Don't misunderstand. I still trust people and I still trust young men. In that sense, I can identify with Barnabas and his natural bent. But I've learned over the years to be more discriminating in appointing leaders. Though my mistakes were painful not only for me, but for others, I've tried to learn and grow in my leadership style—something God wants all of us to do. The apostle Paul certainly has set the example in this area of life.

Principle 2. No matter what our design or our gender, we must allow God's Spirit to conform us into the image of Jesus Christ.

I personally helped to develop a test to determine our God-created design. It's called your Style of Influence (SOI). Not surprisingly, it helps verify that all people have basic traits that are built into our lives from conception. True, our environment molds our personalities to a great extent. But no matter what that influence, it doesn't change our basic design. For example, some people are highly relational by nature. Others are more tough-minded. Some are more abstract in their thinking, and others are more concrete. Still others are highly task-oriented, while others are low task.

The apostle Paul appears to have been rather tough-minded by nature. Though he definitely cared about people, he could be insensitive in his relationships. He was also very task-oriented. Carrying out the Great Commission to preach the gospel to the Gentiles was always at the forefront of his mind. In the process, he at times seemed to step on people's feelings—both Christians and non-Christians. All of these natural tendencies, however, help us understand why God chose Paul for this incredibly difficult task.

Barnabas, on the other hand, had some opposite tendencies. He appears to have been highly relational by nature. Though he may have had a high task orientation like Paul, he could carry out his work in a more sensitive and caring way. This helps explain why he intervened for Paul in Jerusalem and later stood his ground for John Mark—even though he had to confront his best friend. He was consistently concerned for people's feelings.

Though Paul was by nature a more tough-minded person, he nevertheless brought this strength under the powerful influence of the Holy Spirit. Even in his intense and straightforward letter to the Galatians, he spelled out how all Christians ought to relate to one another: "But the fruit of the Spirit," he wrote, "is love, joy, peace, patience, kindness, goodness, faithfulness, gentleness and self-control" (Gal. 5:22–23).

Though it took time for Paul to reflect these qualities in his own life consistently, this was his goal: to be like Jesus Christ. The longer he lived, the more he tempered his natural design with the qualities of godliness.

And so it is with all Christians. *No matter what our design or our gender, we must allow God's Spirit to conform us into the image of Jesus Christ.*[2]

Principle 3. No matter what our failures, either as Christians or non-Christians, God wants to give us a second chance.

Thanks to Barnabas, Mark had a second chance! And thanks to God's grace, Paul had a second chance, not only in his relationship with Timothy, but also in rebuilding a trusting relationship with John Mark. And so it is with us. God wants to give all of us a second, and even a third, and a fourth chance. This is what Christianity is all about!

Don't misunderstand. This does not mean we should ever take advantage of God's grace because of His promise of forgiveness. Every time we fail, we will reap what we sow. The consequences are, of course, determined by the seriousness of our sin. However, God does not want us to wallow in the past. He wants us to experience forgiveness, and like Paul, He wants us to "forget" the past and press on. We serve a God who is even able to take our mistakes and failures and make them work together for good (Rom. 8:28). I can certainly bear witness to this truth in my own life and ministry experience.

Personalizing These Principles

1. As you evaluate your Christian life, do you measure your relationship with Jesus Christ by what you know about the Bible or by the way you live the Christian life?

   God, of course, wants us to keep these traits in balance. That's why Paul wrote to the Ephesians: "I urge you to live a life worthy of the calling you have received" (Eph. 4:1).

   Paul had just spent the first three chapters in this letter outlining the great doctrines of Christianity. In essence, he explained our calling in Christ. He then spent the next three chapters (4–6) outlining how Christians should live their lives in view of this great calling. Read through the Ephesian letter with this thought in mind and then attempt to answer the above question.

2. How would you explain your natural, God-created design? Are you more cognitive or emotional? Are you more tough-minded or sensitive? Are you driven by tasks or by your relationships with people?

   It's important to note that all of us are affected by our environment to one degree or another. For example, if we're highly relational and at the same time insecure, we can become people-pleasers. If we are naturally tough-minded and yet have a lot of repressed anger, we can become very hurtful to others. However, no matter what we are—either by natural design or through environmental influences—the Lord wants us always to reflect the fruit of the Spirit in our relationships with one another. How would you evaluate your life as a Christian in view of what Paul defines as the fruit of the Spirit: "But the fruit of the Spirit is love, joy, peace, patience, kindness, goodness, faithfulness, gentleness and self-control. Against such things there is no law" (Gal. 5:22–23).

3. As you think about your mistakes in life, have you been able to put those things behind you, accept total forgiveness in Christ, and move on in your Christian experience?

It's also important to understand that this involves forgiving those who have sinned against us—perhaps even when we were so young we don't even remember. It's only when we are able to forgive that we are set free from the bondage of anger and hurt. If you can't cross over this line, seek help from an understanding counselor, pastor, or friend. However, don't look for someone who will simply empathize with your problems and never give you instruction and support to make changes in your life.

Set a Goal

As you reflect on the principles that flow from Paul's growth experiences, what one aspect of your life and personality has the Holy Spirit brought to your attention? Set a goal and prayerfully ask the Lord to help you make necessary changes:

_____

_____

_____

_____

Memorize the Following Scripture

Brothers, I do not consider myself yet to have taken hold of it. But one thing I do: Forgetting what is behind and straining toward what is ahead, I press on toward the goal to win the prize for which God has called me heavenward in Christ Jesus.

PHILIPPIANS 3:13–14

Growing Together

1. How would you describe your natural design—your strengths as well as your weaknesses?
2. How has the environment in which you grew up affected your natural design?
3. What changes would you like to make in your natural tendencies in order to reflect the fruit of the Spirit (Gal. 5:22–23)?
4. Would you share with us how you have been able to put the past behind you and have moved on to become a more mature Christian?
5. What can we pray for you specifically?

Chapter 10

A Shepherd's Heart

When Jesus chose a metaphor to describe and illustrate His concern and love for people, He identified Himself as the good shepherd (John 10:11a). He not only knew His sheep but He was willing to die for them (10:11b, 14). He was—and is—the perfect pastor.

Paul modeled his own ministry style after Jesus Christ. In fact, he eventually paid the ultimate price—just as the Savior. However, Paul was only human—and not perfect. Though he was willing to suffer for the cause of Christ from the moment he became a Christian, he did not always exemplify the gentle, caring aspects of his divine model. His zealous, tough-minded approach to defending Pharisaic Judaism carried over into his new passion—to defend the gospel.

However, Paul's goal was to practice what he preached. The more he understood what it meant not only to be "crucified with Christ" but also for Christ to live His life through him (Gal. 2:20), the more he was transformed into Christ's image as a caring and gentle shepherd (Rom. 12:1–2).

We've already seen this beautifully illustrated on his second missionary journey when he and Silas and Timothy ministered in Thessalonica. Using the metaphor of a nursing mother, he fed these believers pure spiritual milk (see 1 Thess. 2:7; 1 Peter 2:2). As they grew and matured in Christ, he then ministered to each believer more deeply, just as "a father deals with his own children, encouraging, comforting and urging" them "to live lives worthy of God" (1 Thess. 2:11–12).

The Third Journey (Acts 18:23–21:16)

Paul's passion for discipling and shepherding believers continued to grow on his third missionary journey. He was deeply concerned that those who were converted to Christ, both on the first and second missionary journeys, continue to grow and mature in their Christian faith. Consequently, he traveled back through Galatia and Phrygia, once again "strengthening all the disciples" (Acts 18:23; see fig. 4).

Don't misunderstand. Paul was always concerned that new believers be grounded in the faith, but this burden grew and intensified as he saw how quickly false teachers could lead his new converts astray. Consequently, Paul increased his efforts to minister to these people at a much more personal level.

The Ephesian Experience (Acts 19:1–20; 20:1)

To understand more fully Paul's shepherd heart, we need to understand his three-year ministry in Ephesus, a major city in Asia. Paul had stopped here briefly on his second journey (see fig. 3, p. 148). But even though his time was short, he used this brief opportunity to evangelize his own people. Luke stated that he "went into the synagogue and reasoned with the Jews" (18:19). We're not told how many became disciples of Jesus Christ but we know he ignited a spark of interest since "they asked him to spend more time with them" (18:20). Paul declined this invitation, but he promised he would return if it was God's will (18:21). The Lord honored Paul's wish and he did return—that time to spend at least three years.

Another Strategic Church (19:1–7)

Paul's follow-up ministry in Ephesus began in a similar way to Peter's initial ministry in Jerusalem. First, approximately twelve men had a unique and powerful encounter with the

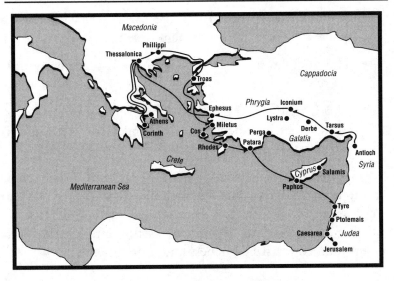

Figure 4
Paul's Third Missionary Journey

Holy Spirit (19:6–7), just as the twelve apostles had in Jerusalem. When Paul arrived on this second visit and met these men, they confessed that they had put their faith in Christ for salvation, but also acknowledged they had not experienced the unique ministry and power of the Holy Spirit. In fact, they had "not even heard that there is a Holy Spirit" (19:2). But when Paul placed his hands on them, "the Holy Spirit came on them, and they spoke in tongues and prophesied" (19:6). In essence, this is what had happened to the apostles years earlier. We can assume that these "twelve men" in Ephesus spoke various languages, just as the Twelve Apostles had done on the day of Pentecost when the Holy Spirit came on them (Acts 1:26–2:15).[1]

This was indeed a unique experience for these twelve men in Ephesus just as it was a unique experience for the Twelve Apostles in Jerusalem. In fact, Luke doesn't even imply that their wives and children had the same experience, let alone others who had put their faith in Christ. You see, God was doing something very special, both in Jerusalem and Ephesus:

- Believers in Jerusalem became the first Jewish church where the Christian movement began.

- The disciples in Antioch became the first major Gentile church.

- The Christians in Ephesus, however, became the first church that included both Jews and Gentiles in significant proportions.[2]

Because the Christians in Ephesus and other cities throughout Asia had this ethnic and religious mix, we can understand more fully why Paul later wrote a circular letter (identified in the New Testament as the letter to the Ephesians) and emphasized oneness and unity in Christ:

> For he himself is our peace, who has made the two one [both Jew and Gentile] and has destroyed the barrier, the dividing wall of hostility, by abolishing in his flesh the law with its commandments and regulations. His purpose was to create in himself one new man out of the two [both Jews and Gentiles], thus making peace, and in this one body to reconcile both of them to God through the cross . . . For through him we both have access to the Father by one Spirit. (Eph. 2:14–16a, 18)

A Fruitful Two Years

Following his initial experience with this small group of men, Paul once again "entered the synagogue" in Ephesus. He "spoke boldly there for three months, arguing persuasively about the kingdom of God" (Acts 19:8). But once again, he faced serious opposition from his Jewish brothers—just as he had experienced in most every other major city on his missionary tours. And once again, he withdrew from the synagogue and expanded his ministry to Gentiles.

To carry on this ministry to both groups, he secured a lecture hall from a man named Tyrannus, perhaps one of the twelve men who had come into a fuller understanding of the gospel and the ministry of the Holy Spirit. There he met daily with all who would listen to his message. Rather than going to them, they came to him—from all over Asia. So many people were exposed to the gospel that Luke has recorded that during this two-year period "all the Jews and Greeks who lived in the province of Asia heard the word of the Lord" (19:10).[3]

Many of those who traveled to Ephesus from their own towns and villages to shop, carry on business, worship in the temple of Diana, and engage in pagan activities also heard about this passionate Jew-turned-Christian who taught daily in Tyrannus's lecture hall. Curious, they stopped by to hear Paul teach and dialogue with his audience. As a result, many became believers and returned to their own cities and started churches, probably in Smyrna, Pergamum, Thyatira, Sardis, Philadelphia, and Laodicea. Along with the church in Ephesus, John refers to these Asian churches in the opening chapters of the Book of Revelation (Rev. 2:1, 8, 12, 18; 3:1, 7, 14, see also fig. 5).

Miraculous Affirmations (Acts 19:11–12)

This unusual response to Paul's message was not only because of what he was preaching and teaching. God enabled him to do "signs, wonders and miracles" to verify the gospel as well as his apostleship (2 Cor. 12:12). Luke has reported: "God did extraordinary miracles through Paul, so that even handkerchiefs and aprons that had touched him were taken to the sick, and their illnesses were cured and the evil spirits left them" (Acts 19:11–12).

The Lord used this Spirit-filled apostle in Ephesus in much the same way as He used Peter in Jerusalem. Identified as "an apostle to the Jews" (Gal. 2:8a), many "people brought the sick into the streets and laid them on beds and mats so that at least Peter's shadow might fall on some of them as he passed by" (Acts 5:15). Just so, God's power was on Paul as an "apostle to the Gentiles" (Gal. 2:8b). The Holy Spirit was not only affirming their divine calling as apostles but also the message they were preaching (Heb. 2:3–4).

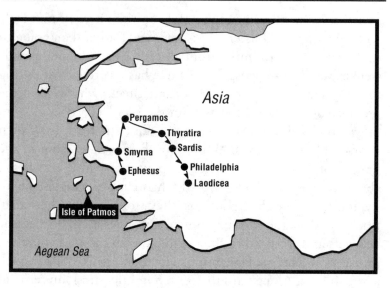

Figure 5
The Seven Churches of Asia

An Ironic Breakthrough (Acts 19:13–16)

There was a major difference, however, between the two environments. Jerusalem was the center of Judaism. God-fearing Jews came from all over the New Testament world to worship the God of Abraham, Isaac, and Jacob. By contrast, Ephesus was a pagan city that was permeated with the occult. People came from all over Asia, and many actually worshiped Satan and evil spirits. In fact, some Jews, who were identified as the "sons of Sceva, a Jewish chief priest," tried to emulate Paul by attempting to cast out spirits in the name of Jesus Christ (19:14). On one occasion, a man possessed by demons jumped on these seven men and overpowered them, beating them so badly "they ran out of the house naked and bleeding" (19:16).

This was such an unusual event that word spread quickly. It impacted both Jews and Gentiles so deeply that an overwhelming fear gripped many of them, particularly those who had indulged in sorcery and other evil activities. Consequently, they did an about-face. Rejecting Satan and his evil cohorts, they confessed their sins and put their faith in Jesus Christ (19:17–18). What makes this ironic is that a demon-possessed man's behavior actually laid the groundwork for a great evangelistic harvest!

A Multimillion-Dollar Bonfire

To demonstrate their new allegiance, these new converts "brought their scrolls together and burned them publicly" (19:19). This created an incredible bonfire and fireworks display that was visible for miles around. Speaking conservatively, by today's standards the cost of these books could have totaled at least five million dollars.[4] You can imagine the impact this had on those who saw and heard about this incredible event. Consequently, "the word of the Lord spread widely and grew in power" (19:20). Thousands became followers of Jesus Christ—just as they had done in Jerusalem (2:41; 4:4; 6:7).

The occult activity in Ephesus also gives us another clue for understanding the content of Paul's letter that he later wrote to this church and the other churches in Asia.[5] Concerned that they not be defeated by Satan—who once controlled their lives—he penned these powerful and encouraging words:

> *Put on the full armor of God so that you can take your stand against the devil's schemes. For our struggle is not against flesh and blood, but against the rulers, against the authorities, against the powers of this dark world and against the spiritual forces of evil in the heavenly realms. Therefore put on the full armor of God, so that when the day of evil comes, you may be able to stand your ground, and after you have done everything, to stand. (Eph. 6:11–13)*

Artemis and Demetrius (Acts 19:23–27)

Not surprisingly, the unusual response to the gospel in Ephesus created jealousy among those who refused to listen to

Paul. In many respects, we see a dramatic replay of what had happened in Jerusalem. In both cities, so many people became Christians it threatened those who had a vested interest in their religion. In Jerusalem, it was the Jewish "high priest and all his associates" (5:17) who became intensely jealous and hostile. In Ephesus, it was a group of pagan businessmen "who made silver shrines of Artemis" (19:24).

Demetrius became a primary mover in reacting to what was happening. This influential entrepreneur had a thriving business as a silversmith that not only serviced those who lived in Ephesus but people throughout Asia. He also employed a number of craftsmen whose income was also affected negatively by the impact of the gospel.

Demetrius called his cohorts together and made a strong emotional appeal on two counts. First, he reported that they would continue to be impacted economically—perhaps even put out of business. They needed to act immediately and decisively and do something about all those people who were worshiping God rather than the goddess Artemis. Second, Demetrius built his appeal on their religious convictions regarding Artemis. Their fertility goddess was in danger of being "robbed of her divine majesty" (19:27).

A Religious Riot (19:28–41)

What happened next also correlates with the Jerusalem experience. Because so many people were becoming Christians in Ephesus and the surrounding regions, the enemies of Christianity initiated a counterattack, accusing Paul on religious grounds. Ironically, when this happened years before in the Holy City, Paul had led the attack in his defense of Judaism. But in Ephesus, he was the object of the attack. Apart from an intervention by the city clerk, the riot that ensued could have taken the lives of many, many believers—including Paul. Fortunately, the Roman government had not given the political leaders in Ephesus the same authority they'd given those who comprised the Jewish Sanhedrin in Jerusalem. Consequently, the city clerk addressed the angry crowd, warning them they could be "charged with rioting"—obviously a serious offense. Fearful that the Roman army might step in to silence them, the crowd gradually dispersed (19:40–41).

Once the people had settled down, Paul met with many of the disciples. He encouraged them in their faith and then left Ephesus and continued on his third journey (see fig. 4, p. 163). It's against this historical backdrop and Paul's dedicated ministry of evangelism and edification in Ephesus, we are now able to get an in-depth look at his "shepherd's heart."

A Meeting in Miletus: A Profile of a Sincere Shepherd (Acts 20:17–38)

Paul's ultimate goal as he continued on his third journey was to return to Jerusalem by the day of Pentecost (Acts 19:21; 20:16)—the very time the Holy Spirit had visited the Twelve Apostles years before and enabled them to launch the first church (Acts 2:1–4). In order to arrive in time, Paul decided "to sail past Ephesus" (20:16). But his heart was still in this Asian city. Apart from his seven-year ministry in Tarsus, he had spent more concentrated time in Ephesus than any other place. Consequently, when his ship docked at Miletus (see fig. 4, p. 163), he sent a message to the elders in Ephesus and requested that they meet him there. It was a deeply moving reunion and gives us a clear and touching portrait of Paul the shepherd—not just the evangelist and theologian.

Unselfish and Compassionate

> *I served the Lord with great humility and with tears . . . . Remember that for three years I never stopped warning each of you night and day with tears. (Acts 20:19a, 31b)*

In many respects, this is a different Paul than the one we encountered in the early years of his ministry. He has deepened and mellowed, particularly in his relationship with people. His compassion often caused him to weep.

Don't misunderstand. Paul was still very intense and driven by the task God called him to fulfill. He never changed that pattern until the day God took him home to heaven. But like all of us who grow and mature, he reflected more and more the fruit of the Holy Spirit in all of his relationships. In fact, he more and more practiced what he preached (see Gal. 5:22–23)—a mark of a great man of God.

Unintimidated and Uncompromising

You know that I have not hesitated to preach anything that would be helpful to you but have taught you publicly and from house to house. . . . For I have not hesitated to proclaim to you the whole will of God. (Acts 20:20, 27)

As Paul developed into a sensitive shepherd, he never lost his boldness. He simply balanced more and more his tendency to be direct and to the point with compassion and gentleness. He never compromised his message because of fear or to avoid rejection. He taught the "whole counsel of God." Moreover, Paul became a man who was "able to teach"—a character quality he looked for in elders (1 Tim. 3:2).

What does it mean "to be able to teach"? Paul defined this character quality for Timothy in his final letter and cautioned him to avoid "foolish and stupid arguments." Becoming even more specific, he said that "the Lord's servant must not quarrel; instead, he must be kind to everyone, able to teach, not resentful" (2 Tim. 2:23–24).

But what about those people who will oppose us as we attempt to proclaim the Word of God? Paul answered this question in the same paragraph when he wrote that we "must gently instruct" these people—"in the hope that God will grant them repentance leading them to a knowledge of the truth" (2:25).

This is also why Paul later wrote to the Ephesians from a Roman prison and exhorted them always to speak "the truth in love" (Eph. 4:15). He had demonstrated this quality of life when he ministered among them. Consequently, he had earned the right to exhort them.

Unprejudiced and Impartial (Acts 20:21)

I have declared to both Jews and Greeks that they must turn to God in repentance and have faith in our Lord Jesus. (Acts 20:21)

Paul learned quickly that Jesus Christ died for all people. He was not just a Jewish Savior. There was "one flock and one shepherd" (John 10:16). Jesus had made this point clear to the other apostles when He stated that He had "other sheep that are not of" the Jewish "sheep pen" (10:16). However, they were so prejudiced at that point in time that Jesus' words went in one ear and out the other. As we've noted before, it took Peter at least five years after the birth of the church in Jerusalem to truly understand "that God does not show favoritism but accepts men from every nation who fear him and do what is right" (Acts 10:34–35).

After Paul's conversion on the road to Damascus, he very quickly began to comprehend his prejudice, not only against Gentiles but many of his fellow Jews who had become Christians. When he was led blind into the city of Damascus and received his "physical sight" three days later, he also received "spiritual sight" that even the apostles in Jerusalem had not understood. He was God's "chosen instrument" to carry Christ's name "before the Gentiles" (Acts 9:15).

From this point forward, Paul's very narrow view of God's eternal plans expanded to include all people, regardless of their racial and cultural backgrounds. He made this crystal clear in the first letter he ever wrote when he stated without equivocation: "You are all sons of God through faith in Christ Jesus, for all of you who were baptized into Christ have clothed yourselves with Christ. There is neither Jew nor Greek, slave nor free, male nor female, for you are all one in Christ Jesus" (Gal. 3:26–28).

Sacrificial and Dedicated

> *I consider my life worth nothing to me, if only I may finish the race and complete the task the Lord Jesus has given me—the task of testifying to the gospel of God's grace. (Acts 20:24)*

These were not only words for Paul. He meant what he shared with the Ephesian elders. He had already proven his point, even when he faced the riot in Ephesus. But he would have more opportunities ahead of him—more so than he realized.

During his first imprisonment in Rome, he demonstrated the same sacrificial attitude in his letter to the Philippians: "I eagerly expect and hope that I will in no way be ashamed, but will have sufficient courage so that now as always Christ will be exalted in my body, whether by life or by death. For to me, to live is Christ and to die is gain" (Phil. 1:20–21).

During Paul's second imprisonment, which was far more difficult and serious since he was chained in a Roman dungeon rather than in his "own rented house" (Acts 28:30), he penned some of his final words before he was executed. He was about to live out in a very specific way what he had shared with the Ephesian elders that day in Miletus:

> *For I am already being poured out like a drink offering, and the time has come for my departure. I have fought the good fight, I have finished the race, I have kept the faith. Now there is in store for me the crown of righteousness, which the Lord, the righteous Judge, will award to me on that day—and not only to me, but also to all who have longed for his appearing. (2 Tim. 4:6–8)*

Accountable and Pastoral (Acts 20:28)

> *Keep watch over yourselves and all the flock of which the Holy Spirit has made you overseers. Be shepherds of the church of God, which he bought with his own blood. (Acts 20:28).*

Paul knew how easy it is to lose focus in the ministry. He also knew the power of the flesh and how vulnerable we are to being led astray, even as spiritual leaders. To guard against Satan's evil attacks, he taught that we all need accountability, both as shepherds and as members of Christ's body at large. This is why he warned the Ephesian elders that even among them were men who would attempt to "distort the truth in order to draw away disciples after them" (20:30). But he also knew that "savage wolves" would infiltrate the church with no regard for the "flock" of God (20:29).

"Be on your guard," Paul warned (20:31)—a relevant message to all Christians today, to both leaders and to those who follow. Paul had modeled this behavior as a shepherd when he ministered among them for three years. And now he could say without fear of contradiction, "I never stopped warning each of you night and day with tears" (20:31).

Not Covetous and Generous (20:33–35)

> *I have not coveted anyone's silver or gold or clothing. You yourselves know that these hands of mine have supplied my own needs and the needs of my companions. In everything I did, I showed you that by this kind of hard work we must help the weak, remembering the words the Lord Jesus himself said: "It is more blessed to give than to receive." (Acts 20:33–35)*

Paul was above reproach when it came to finances. If he thought anyone would misinterpret his motives, he would not receive material gifts. He made this point clear in several of his letters, but never more clear than in his first epistle to the Thessalonians. With deep conviction, he wrote: "Surely you remember, brothers, our toil and hardship; we worked night and day in order not to be a burden to anyone while we preached the gospel of God to you" (1 Thess. 2:9).

This does not mean Paul did not accept money and other material gifts from Christians. In fact, while he was laboring so diligently in Thessalonica and not accepting financial support, he was at the same time, accepting gifts from the Christians in Philippi (Phil. 4:15–16).

Why this difference? The answer is clear if you understand his ministry approach. On the one hand, he believed whole-heartedly that "elders who direct the affairs of the church well are worthy of double honor, especially those whose work is preaching and teaching" (1 Tim. 5:17). The term *double honor* is definitely a word for material support. Paul was simply teaching what Jesus taught—that "the worker deserves his wages" (1 Tim. 5:18).

But on the other hand, Paul also believed in going the extra mile to avoid being accused of taking advantage of people financially. In fact, at times he did not receive support when he was entitled to it. This happened in Corinth which is clearly mentioned in his first letter to these believers (1 Cor. 9:1–15). "If others have this right of support from you, shouldn't we have it all the more? But," he stated, "we did not use this right" (1 Cor. 9:12). The reason, of course, is clear. Paul did not want to be accused of ministering merely for money.

Again Paul practiced what he preached when he ministered in Ephesus. And when he later wrote to Timothy who was helping establish the church in Ephesus, he cautioned this young man only to appoint an elder who was "hospitable" and "not a lover of money" (1 Tim. 3:2–3).

Becoming God's Man Today

Principles to Live By

Paul's shepherding model touches all of us, whether pastor, parent, employer, or neighbor. The following principles flow from his example in the Book of Acts and also from the letters he wrote:

Principle 1. To be effective in communicating God's truth to others, we must model God's truth.

Though "what we are" as Christians is inseparably linked to "what we say," it is foundational. It gives meaning and validity to our words. This is why Paul could write to the Corinthians and the Thessalonians and say:

- *Follow my example, as I follow the example of Christ. (1 Cor. 11:1)*

- *You are witnesses, and so is God, of how holy, righteous and blameless we were among you who believed. (1 Thess. 2:10)*

Significantly, Paul's reference to modeling in his letter to the Thessalonians is in the very context where he used the "mother-father" metaphors to illustrate his own ministry. This indicates how much Paul believed that modeling is foundational in the communication process beginning with parent-child relationships.

Years ago, a British psychologist, Dr. J. H. Hadfield, made a startling statement that grabbed my attention. Though a secularist, he had captured a biblical truth. "We see," he wrote, "that it is by a perfectly natural process that the child develops standards of behavior in a moral sense. So that if you never taught a child one single moral maxim, he would nevertheless develop moral—or immoral—standards of right and wrong by the process of identification."[6]

Hadfield's conclusion correlates beautifully with biblical truth. The lesson is clear. If we want our children to "love as Christ loved," we must not just *tell* them to "love as Christ loved." Rather, we must "love as Christ loved." If we want them to pray, *we* must pray. If we want them to be kind to others, *we* must be kind to others. If we want them to share their faith, *we* must share *our* faith. If we want them to read their Bibles, *we* must read *our* Bibles.

This modeling principle is particularly applicable to those of us who are fathers. Since God is identified in Scripture as "our heavenly Father," the only way children comprehend what the invisible God is like is to see "God in us." If what we see in our lives does not match up with what God is really like, they will develop a distorted view of who He really is.

I learned this lesson in a new way when I once overheard my two daughters (now grown but then about ages four and five) having a discussion. Suddenly the younger had a stroke of insight. "Hey," she said to her older sister, "God is our heavenly Daddy." I'll never forget that statement. Though they didn't know I was listening, their conversation impacted my life. You see, my daughters' view of me was their view of God. It's an awesome thought and a tremendous responsibility.

This principle certainly applies in a very special way to all of us who are spiritual leaders. This is why Paul used the family structure as a means for evaluating a man's qualifications for pastoral leadership in the church. Writing to Timothy while he was in Ephesus, Paul said: "He must manage his own family well and see that his children obey him with proper respect. (If anyone does not know how to manage his own family, how can he take care of God's church?)" (1 Tim. 3:4–5).

Here the word *manage* refers to being a good shepherd—a person who really cares for his sheep, whether they are our literal children or our spiritual children. Paul, of course, has modeled what this means in his conversation with the Ephesian elders.

Principle 2. All Christians should set their hearts on reflecting the qualifications Paul outlined for being good shepherds of God's people.

When Paul wrote to Timothy and Titus, he specified a number of qualities that should characterize those who are selected for eldership in the church (1 Tim. 3:1–7; Titus 1:5–9). When these characteristics are combined, the list is as follows:

1. Above reproach (having a good reputation)
2. Husband of one wife (maintaining moral purity)
3. Temperate (exemplifying balance in words and actions)

4. Prudent (being wise and humble)
5. Respectable (serving as a good role model)
6. Hospitable (demonstrating unselfishness and generosity)
7. Able to teach (communicating sensitively in a nonthreatening and nondefensive manner)
8. Not given to wine (not being addicted to substances)
9. Not self-willed (not being a self-centered and controlling personality)
10. Not quick-tempered (void of anger that becomes sinful)
11. Not pugnacious (not an abusive person)
12. Uncontentious (nonargumentative and nondivisive)
13. Gentle (a sensitive, loving, and kind person)
14. Free from the love of money (nonmaterialistic)
15. One who manages his own household well (a good husband and father)
16. A good reputation with those outside the church (a good testimony to unbelievers)
17. Love what is good (pursuing godly activities)
18. Just (wise, discerning, nonprejudiced, and fair)
19. Devout (holy and righteous)
20. Not a new convert (not a new Christian)[7]

After serving as a professor for twenty years, I became a church-planting pastor. When I helped launch the first Fellowship Bible Church in Dallas, Texas, I began meeting with a group of approximately twenty-five men every Thursday morning for Bible study and prayer. I suggested to these men that we take one of the above qualities each week, discuss its meaning from Scripture, and then share with each other how we could develop this quality in our lives.

But, someone might say, these are qualities for spiritual leaders. This is true. Paul was simply saying that if a man wants to be a spiritual leader, this is a wonderful goal. However, he was instructing Timothy and Titus to make sure that these men were spiritual and mature. He then outlined a profile for evaluating that maturity.

Interestingly, Paul mentions these qualities in other portions of Scripture where he describes all Christians. In these passages in 1 Timothy and Titus, he simply pulls together all of those qualities into two very comprehensive profiles. In other words, these qualities should be goals for all believers. They are what makes a man a good husband, a good father, a good employer or employee, and a good neighbor—not just a good pastor with a shepherd's heart.

Personalizing These Principles

Utilizing the qualities exemplified by Paul in his conversation with the Ephesian elders (pp. 169–174) as well as the qualities he outlined in his letters to Timothy and Titus, evaluate your own life as a Christian (pp. 176–177). Check (√) those you feel good about. Circle those you'd like to set as goals to develop a more biblical shepherd's heart.

Set a Goal

It's important at this point not to let this assignment discourage you. Paul has set a very high standard for all of us. In your desire to develop a shepherd's heart, ask the Holy Spirit to impress on your mind just one area for change. Then use that quality to set a goal, asking God to help you make changes in your life:

_____

_____

_____

Memorize the Following Scripture

You were taught, with regard to your former way of life,
to put off your old self, which is being corrupted by its deceitful desires;
to be made new in the attitude of your minds; and to put on the new self,
created to be like God in true righteousness and holiness.
EPHESIANS 4:22–24

Growing Together

1. From your own experience, share why "modeling" is such a foundational concept in Christian communication.
2. How has positive Christian modeling impacted your own life? By contrast, how has negative modeling impacted your own life?
3. As you've reflected on Paul's personal example and the instructions in his letters to Timothy and Titus, would you feel free to share the one goal you have set for your life?
4. When we look over this very high standard in Scripture, how can we be challenged rather than become discouraged?
5. What can we pray for you specifically?

Chapter 11

Decisions That Determined Destiny

*H*ave you ever heard Christian leaders teach that God's perfect will for His children always involves freedom from physical pain, emotional struggles, and spiritual battles? Paul's dedicated life as a Christian certainly demonstrates that this is false doctrine. His decision to go to Jerusalem was definitely God's perfect will for him, but the results were anything but pleasant. In fact, he almost lost his life. His physical pain was excruciating, his emotional agony was almost unbearable, and his spiritual struggles were against Satan himself.

A Settled Decision (Acts 19:21)

Just prior to the huge uproar and riot in Ephesus, Paul unequivocally "decided to go to Jerusalem" (Acts 19:21). Though he had been hoping to make this trip from the moment he launched out on his third missionary journey, he settled on the specific time frame toward the end of his three-year ministry in this key Asian city.

Paul made his primary objective for this trip very clear. He wanted to deliver gifts of money to needy Christians. He knew that a number of believers in the Jerusalem area had some desperate physical needs and he wanted to help them. He had never forgotten the day in Jerusalem when the apostles—Peter and

John particularly—had affirmed his ministry to the Gentiles with a very important request. "They agreed that we should go to the Gentiles, and they to the Jews," he wrote to the Galatians. "All they asked was that we should continue to remember the poor, the very thing I was eager to do" (Gal. 2:9–10).

But Paul had several related objectives that are more subtle but also clear. True, he wanted to demonstrate to the Jewish Christians in Jerusalem, the leaders particularly, that he had not forgotten their charge. But more importantly, he wanted them to know that he had taught his pagan converts that they owed a debt of gratitude to Jewish believers. Consequently, as Paul continued on his third missionary journey and revisited Thessalonica and Corinth (see fig. 4, p. 163), he informed the Christians in these cities about this urgent need. In fact, he communicated very directly that these believers had an obligation to their Jewish brothers and sisters. If it had not been for the apostles' charge to Paul and Barnabas to go to the Gentiles, the gospel might never have penetrated their pagan world (see Rom. 15:25–27).

Paul's Letter to the Christians in Rome

When Paul arrived in Corinth, he penned a letter to the believers in Rome—one of his most comprehensive epistles. Though he had never been to the capital city, he was acquainted with a number of Christians who lived there (Rom. 16:1–15). He had wanted to visit them for years and planned to stop by on his way to Spain (Rom. 15:23–24). But first, he let them know he was headed for Jerusalem to carry out his very specific purpose:

> *Now, however, I am on my way to Jerusalem in the service of the saints there. For Macedonia and Achaia were pleased to make a contribution for the poor among the saints in Jerusalem. They were pleased to do it, and indeed they owe it to them. For if the Gentiles have shared in the Jews' spiritual blessings, they*

owe it to the Jews to share with them their material blessings.
(Rom. 15:25–27)

Paul's Letter to the Christians in Corinth

As Paul traveled and shared this special need, the Gentile
believers in Macedonia and Achaia were eager to participate,
not only because of a sense of indebtedness, but out of sincere
gratitude. In fact, the Macedonians—who certainly included
the Philippians, the Bereans, and the Thessalonians—modeled
generosity for believers of all time. Paul was so impressed with
their sacrificial attitudes that he spelled it out in detail in his
second letter to the Corinthians—believers who were faltering
in their faith promises to participate in this project:

> *And now, brothers, we want you to know about the grace that*
> *God has given the Macedonian churches. Out of the most severe*
> *trial, their overflowing joy and their extreme poverty welled up in*
> *rich generosity. For I testify that they gave as much as they were*
> *able, and even beyond their ability. Entirely on their own, they*
> *urgently pleaded with us for the privilege of sharing in this service*
> *to the saints. (2 Cor. 8:1–4)*

Here again, Paul's reference to the "saints" in this paragraph
referred to the poor Jewish Christians in Jerusalem. Eventually
the Corinthians—who were noted for their lack of spiritual
depth—also responded, but not until they had had several
reminders and a great deal of accountability (2 Cor. 9:6–8).
With the assistance of several men appointed by the various
churches, Paul collected the money and continued on his way to
Jerusalem.

Paul's Commitment to Accountability

Paul never handled these money gifts alone—lest he be
accused of "putting his hand in the till." As we've seen in his

meeting with the Ephesian elders, he wanted to be above reproach, never giving people an opportunity to accuse him of "loving money" or stealing it. Consequently, as he collected these monetary gifts, he had the churches in every major area appoint trustworthy men to travel with him. In fact, this is such an important factor that the Holy Spirit spelled out who these men were and where they were from. Paul "was accompanied by Sopater son of Pyrrhus from Berea, Aristarchus and Secundus from Thessalonica, Gaius from Derbe, Timothy also, and Tychicus and Trophimus from the province of Asia" (Acts 20:4). It seems apparent that these men—as a team—travelled with Paul and transported these gifts of money to Jerusalem where they deposited it with the elders.[1]

This is a very important principle for Christian leaders today. In our own church, none of our pastors or even the lay elders count or deposit the money. We have other qualified teams count the offering, record the amounts, and immediately lock these funds plus the written records in keyless bags. These containers are then given to another team in the office who have keys to open the bags. The funds are once again counted and the totals are compared with the original records. All the funds are then deposited in a bank. All check numbers and amounts are recorded with the names of the donors and reported to these people quarterly.

As a further precaution against misuse of funds, every check that is written out of the church account must have two authorized signatures. As a final step, a detailed report is given to the elders once a month as to all income and expenditures. We can never be too careful in applying this biblical principle that was exemplified by Paul throughout his ministry.

Mixed Messages

There is no question that Paul believed it was God's will for him to make this trip to Jerusalem. However, he knew he would face some serious and threatening challenges, which he also mentioned in his letter to the Romans. Consequently, he shared two specific prayer requests.

Paul's Personal Petitions

> *Pray that I may be rescued from the unbelievers in Judea.*
> (Rom. 15:31a)

Paul knew from personal experience how hostile many of these Jews could be who had not responded to the gospel. And as we've seen throughout his life's story, Paul was continually persecuted by his own people. Often they tried to take his life. Furthermore, at one time, he had been one of them, persecuting Christians—even putting them to death.

> *Pray that . . . my service in Jerusalem may be acceptable to the saints there. (15:31b)*

Paul wasn't sure how the elders would respond to his efforts to bring money to help the poor among them. He knew how prejudiced his own people could be. Strict Jews refused to receive financial help from Gentiles—and these attitudes often continued to permeate the Jewish church.

This shouldn't surprise us in view of Peter's lingering prejudice before his encounter with Cornelius. Spiritual pride can be deeply ingrained in our souls. Furthermore, some close-knit people at times refuse to do things they would ordinarily do simply because of the fallout and rejection they would feel from others who disagree. Paul was concerned about these intense emotional dynamics—and that's why he requested prayer that the gift might "be acceptable to the saints."

The Spirit's Warnings

In addition to his own premonitions about the difficulties he might face in Jerusalem, Paul received very specific and repeated warnings directly from the Holy Spirit about the way he would be treated when he arrived. He shared this information with the Ephesian elders when he met with them in Miletus. First, he told them he was "compelled by the Spirit," to go "to Jerusalem." However, the same Holy Spirit warned him in city after city that he would face "prison and hardships" (Acts 20:22–23).

The mixed message is obvious. He was definitely in God's perfect will in making this decision. But the Holy Spirit also stated unequivocally that he would face serious persecution. Though the message was mixed, it was not contradictory. The only people who were confused were other Christians—not Paul himself. He knew what he had to do, even if he lost his life (20:22–24).

These prophetic utterances continued after Paul left Miletus. During his seven-day stay with the disciples in Tyre, he received the same divine message: "Through the Spirit they urged Paul not to go on to Jerusalem" (21:4).

The Prophet Agabus

This supernatural message was even more specific and dramatic the closer he came to Jerusalem. When Paul and his entourage came to Caesarea, we once again meet Agabus—a prophet who had years earlier "stood up" in the church in Antioch "and through the Spirit predicted that a severe famine would spread over the entire Roman world" (11:28). As prophesied, it happened, and it was Paul—along with Barnabas—who delivered money gifts from the church in Antioch to meet the needs of the Christians in Judea (11:29). And now, years later, Paul was on his way to Jerusalem with a group of men to carry out the same purpose. As before, Agabus "came down from Judea" and prophesied. Luke, who was a part of Paul's traveling team, has given us both an eye- and ear-witness account:

After we had been there a number of days, a prophet named Agabus came down from Judea. Coming over to us, he took Paul's belt, tied his own hands and feet with it and said,

"The Holy Spirit says, 'In this way the Jews of Jerusalem will bind the owner of this belt and will hand him over to the Gentiles.'" (Acts 21:10–11)

When the Christians at Caesarea heard this prophecy, they "pleaded with Paul not to go up to Jerusalem"—which is understandable (21:12). They were frightened and fearful, and wept over what they knew would come to pass. Agabus had proven himself a true prophet of God—and they had no doubts about the validity of his message.

Though touched by their concerns, Paul remained steadfast in his determination to continue his journey. "Why are you weeping and breaking my heart?" he responded. Even though he knew he was going to face serious conflict, he also knew that he had a divine appointment in Jerusalem. His response to their tearful pleas settled the issue: "'I am ready not only to be bound, but also to die in Jerusalem for the name of the Lord Jesus'" (21:13).

When the Caesarean Christians heard this determined response from their beloved friend and brother, they "gave up and said, 'the Lord's will be done'" (21:14). They knew Paul well enough to conclude that further dialogue would be totally nonproductive. Even though the Holy Spirit chose to give them some very realistic and distressful information, they also knew that the Lord was leading Paul to continue toward his destination. The message was mixed, but the source was God Himself.

Dramatic Scenes in Jerusalem

A Meeting with the Elders (21:15–20a)

When Paul arrived in Jerusalem, he wasted no time in making contact with the spiritual leaders in the church. After staying overnight in the home of Mnason and experiencing wonderful hospitality, he and his companions met with

"James, and all the elders" the very "next day" (21:16–17). Paul shared in detailed fashion his ministry "among the Gentiles" and how these pagans had responded to the gospel. Though Luke doesn't mention specifically that it was at this time that Paul presented the gifts of money for the poor, we can assume it happened at this very moment. After all, this was one of Paul's primary reasons for coming to Jerusalem.

We can also assume that the elders received the gift with gratitude since Luke, who was witnessing everything that was happening, has recorded that "when they heard" Paul's report regarding the Gentiles' response to the gospel, "they praised God" (21:20). In fact, Paul's earlier prayer requests outlined in his letter to the Romans were answered. As they laid what must have been multiple bags of money at the feet of the elders in Jerusalem, it definitely became "material proof" that Gentiles throughout the Roman world were truly converted to Jesus Christ. Nothing demonstrates true commitment more than generosity.

Good News, Bad News

As encouraging as this "praise service" must have been for Paul, he was about to face some stinging disappointments. The tone of the meeting changed quickly—which may have been one reason why Luke has given so little time and space to recording the elders' response to Paul's detailed report and gifts. These men were very concerned about the attitudes some of their fellow believers had about Paul. "'You see brother,'" they said, "'how many thousands of Jews have believed, and all of them are zealous for the law'" (21:20). But what must have been most disturbing to Paul had to be their next statement: "They have been informed that you teach all the Jews who live among the Gentiles to turn away from Moses, telling them not to circumcise their children or live according to our customs" (21:21).

These conclusions were simply rumors. Paul had not taught Jews to stop circumcising their children. In fact, when

Timothy, whose mother was a Jewess and whose father was a Gentile, decided to join Paul's missionary team, he had this young man circumcised in order to enable him to communicate more effectively the gospel to the Jews (Acts 16:3).

On the other hand, it's true that Paul had taught emphatically that no one could inherit eternal life by practicing circumcision or keeping any other aspect of the Mosaic law. Salvation comes by grace through faith. In other matters, however, Paul exercised his freedom to "become all things to all men so that by all possible means" he "might save some" (1 Cor. 9:22). In fact, "to the Jews" he "became like a Jew, to win the Jews" (9:20).

A Plan That Backfired (21:20b–26)

James and the other elders put the question squarely to Paul, reflecting their own fear. "'What shall we do?'" they queried. "'They will certainly hear that you have come'" (Acts 21:22).

Evidently not waiting for Paul's response, they answered their own question. "'Do what we tell you,'" they hastily continued. They remembered that four Jewish Christians had made a vow and were about to go through a period of purification. They insisted that Paul join these men in these rites and even "pay their expenses" (21:24).

Paul was in a difficult spot. He saw the fear in his brothers' eyes and heard the urgency in their voices. Consequently, he decided to take their advice—which was in harmony with his personal freedom to practice his Jewishness without compromising the Christian gospel of salvation by grace.

Unfortunately, from a human point of view, the plan backfired. A number of Jews who had rejected Jesus Christ as the Messiah and Savior had come "from the province of Asia," obviously to participate in the feast of Pentecost (21:27). They recognized Paul, no doubt having heard him speak in Ephesus during the three-year period he was there. In fact, they may have been among those who had initially rejected Paul's message in the synagogue and then had witnessed his productive ministry in the school of Tyrannus (19:8–10). They may have also been among those who had joined in the riot following the great bonfire when so many Jews and Gentiles had burned their occult books. Ironically, they were about to be a part of another riot—one that would turn out far differently than the one in Ephesus. At that time, Paul had escaped unharmed, but this time he was about to be incarcerated, just as the Holy Spirit had revealed all along the way.

Trophimus the Ephesian (21:27–29)

What had irritated these men the most was that they had seen Paul with "Trophimus the Ephesian," one of his traveling companions. Because of their extreme prejudice against Paul, they reported that he had taken this man into the temple area (21:29).

Had this been true, it would have been a serious violation of Jewish law. Gentiles could enter the "outer court"—the place where Jesus encountered the money-changers—but they could *never* cross over into the inner court. To do so was punishable by death. The Roman government had authorized the Sanhedrin to carry out this punishment against any Gentile who had violated this restriction.

If Paul had indeed taken Trophimus into this "sacred place"—which he had not—he would have been guilty of violating this Jewish law. Accusing him falsely, this group of Asian Jews seized Paul, shouting indictments against him. Unfortunately, the crowds believed them and "the whole city was aroused, and the people came running from all directions" (21:30).

Paul Attacked and Rescued (21:30–36)

The scene turned nasty and ugly, just as it had so many years ago when Paul had overseen Stephen's death. This time, Paul was the one who was the object of Jewish hostility. Crowds of people surrounded him after he had been dragged bodily from the temple area. They had one objective in mind: to take Paul's life (21:31)!

These angry people would have succeeded in beating Paul to death if a group of Roman soldiers had not intervened. Confused and bewildered by what was happening, the Roman commander attempted to maneuver Paul into the Roman garrison where they could at least have a reasonable conversation.

Paul's Public Defense (21:37–22:29)

At this point, Paul, already bruised and bleeding, asked if he could address the crowd. Granted permission, he spoke in Aramaic, the language spoken by Judean Jews. Hearing their own native tongue, the crowd suddenly grew quiet. They listened intently to Paul as he shared his educational background, particularly his studies with Gamaliel, a name that brought feelings of great esteem. They even listened to Paul share his conversion story that took place on the road to Damascus. But when he told them about the Lord's call on his life to preach the gospel to the Gentiles, they once again erupted, this time with even more intensity and fury (22:22–23).

Totally unaware of Paul's unique background, the Roman commander simply assumed he had committed some horrible crime. How could these people be so terribly out of control if he hadn't? Consequently, he once again ordered that Paul be taken inside the Roman garrison—this time to be flogged and interrogated!

This procedure was customary in both Greece and Rome in order to get a criminal to confess. It was a horrible experience—a means of torture that could leave a person maimed for life. If prolonged, it could mean death.

Paul was keenly aware of what was happening. If the commander's orders were carried out, his ministry would be over. Apart from a miracle healing, Paul knew he could have died in the very place where he had caused so many deaths.

Don't misunderstand. Paul was ready to give his life for his faith, as he had testified in Caesarea (21:13). However, he sensed that God still had some unique plans for him. Consequently, he cried out that he was a Roman citizen, knowing it was against Roman law to flog a man who had not been duly tried. The plan worked and Paul was allowed to appear before the Jewish Sanhedrin.

A Jewish Conspiracy (22:30–23:22)

How ironic! Before Paul was converted years ago, another man had stood before this group of powerful men. His name was Stephen, and he had been sentenced to death for blasphemy. Since Paul had supervised Stephen's execution, imagine the memories that must have flooded his soul!

From a human point of view, appearing before the Sanhedrin was more threatening and dangerous than being incarcerated by the Romans. Prejudice, pride, and hostility permeated these men's hearts. But they couldn't agree among themselves and the scene became so violent, the Roman commander feared that "Paul would be torn to pieces by them" (23:10). Consequently, he ordered that Paul once again be taken into Roman custody.

Angered even more, a group numbering forty men "formed a conspiracy and bound themselves with an oath not to eat or drink until they had killed Paul" (23:12). They even presented their strategy to the Sanhedrin, who agreed to this evil plan and consented to set up Paul (23:15). However, the Lord had already reassured His servant that he would not face death in Jerusalem. Rather, he would also have the opportunity to testify about Jesus Christ in Rome (23:11).

Transported to Caesarea

True to His word, the Lord delivered Paul. He used Paul's nephew—the son of Paul's sister—to expose this plot. This young man got word regarding what was happening and relayed the information to Paul, who sent him to the commander. This Roman leader, in turn, arranged for Paul to be transported to Caesarea, where he would appear before a Roman governor named Felix (23:16–24).

Paul was very disappointed with this turn of events in Jerusalem. Though he had expected trouble, he had certainly hoped for a more positive response to the gospel among his fellow Jews. After all, he had been one of them. Perhaps he thought they would have listened to his personal testimony. But his hopes were dashed when the crowd so quickly rejected his witness and the men in the Sanhedrin actually cooperated with the plot to take his life.

But Paul's disappointments became God's opportunities. Paul had planned on visiting Rome and now he was about to make that journey—not as a free man as he had hoped but as a prisoner. But he *was* on his way. Little did he realize that the trip would take over two years. However, he would have a great opportunity to present the gospel to many people, including high-ranking Roman officials—just as God had revealed this truth to Ananias shortly after Paul was converted on the road to Damascus (9:15–16).

Appearance Before Felix (24:1–27)

Paul first appeared before Felix, the governor of Judea. Years earlier, another man had appeared before another governor of Judea. The governor's name was Pontius Pilate and the accused was Jesus Christ. As Paul stood before Felix, he certainly reflected on that event. As far as we know, he had not witnessed that terrible moment in history. He was a dedicated Pharisee living in Tarsus and propagating the Mosaic Law and all of the Pharisaical codes he had learned from Gamaliel. At that time, he had had no love whatsoever for this Galilean who claimed to be the Messiah. Now he was standing before Felix as a devoted follower of the One he had rejected.

Paul's accusers came from Jerusalem and charged him with desecrating the temple, an outright lie (24:6). Paul made a noble defense, denying these charges, but openly admitted his relationship with Jesus Christ (24:10–16). When it came to his personal faith, he never compromised.

Sensing there was no real evidence against Paul, but expecting Paul to bribe him, Felix delayed making a decision (24:26). He had probably heard about the enormous sums of money Paul delivered to the Jewish elders and falsely assumed that he was a wealthy religious fanatic. Consequently, he kept Paul under guard for two years, but gave him more freedom than the average prisoner—no doubt, part of his plan to manipulate Paul for material gain (24:23). In his heart, Felix knew this man was innocent, just as Pilate knew Jesus Christ was innocent. But like Pilate, he succumbed to political pressure. In fact, even when Felix was replaced by Porcius Festus, he left Paul incarcerated in order "to grant a favor to the Jews" (24:27).

Appearance Before Festus (25:1–12)

Festus was also partial to the Jews. Consequently, he asked Paul if he would "be willing to go up to Jerusalem" and stand trial before him there—no doubt, before the Sanhedrin (25:9). Paul knew instantly that the deck would be stacked against him. Consequently, he once more used his rights as a Roman citizen—this time to "appeal to Caesar" (25:11).

Paul may have also reasoned that he had already appeared before these men to present the gospel of Jesus Christ. They rejected his message, even plotting to kill him. As in every city Paul had gone, once rejected by the Jews, he turned to the Gentiles. This had now happened in Jerusalem. Paul's conscience was clear. He had testified for Christ at the very center of Judaism and before the most powerful Jewish leaders in the world.

Appearance Before Agrippa (25:13–26, 32)

Before Paul was transported on his way to Rome, he had the opportunity to give another wonderful testimony—this time before King Agrippa while Festus listened in. Though

Festus concluded that Paul was out of his mind because of his academic studies, Agrippa assessed the situation much more objectively. "'This man could have been set free if he had not appealed to Caesar,'" he concluded (26:32).

Though things were not turning out as he had hoped, Paul knew in his heart he was in God's perfect will. Perhaps he reflected on the words he had already written to the Christians in Rome: "And we know that in all things God works for the good of those who love him, who have been called according to his purpose" (Rom. 8:28).

Becoming God's Man Today

Principles to Live By

There are many principles that flow from Paul's life as he entered this phase of his missionary career. Following, however, are two great biblical truths that will help all of us face difficulties with greater understanding and endurance.

Principle 1. Living in God's good, acceptable, and perfect will doesn't guarantee freedom from environmental crises that cause physical pain, emotional struggles, and spiritual battles (1 Peter 1:6–7).

Once Paul became a Christian, he faced incredible difficulties that lasted most of his ministry life. Often he and his missionary companions "felt the sentence of death" (2 Cor. 1:9). Yet Paul knew they were in the perfect will of God.

This is a very important principle since there are Christian leaders today who teach that it is God's will that we experience freedom from illness, have material prosperity, and enjoy all of the things that go along with the so-called "good life." To paraphrase one televangelist, "We are God's kids, and He wants us to have everything—good health, lots of money, and a lavish lifestyle. After all, God owns it all, and He wants us to take possession of the land."

If this were true, why did the apostles suffer and die without these things? Why did many New Testament Christians have to give their lives for what they believed? "Some faced jeers and flogging, while still others were chained and put in prison. They were stoned; they were sawed in two; they were put to death by the sword. They went about in sheepskins and goatskins, destitute, persecuted and mistreated" (Heb. 11:36–37).

Fortunately, most of us have never faced this kind of persecution because we're Christians. In fact, God's will generally is that we be able to "live peaceful and quiet lives in all godliness and holiness" (1 Tim. 2:2). This is why Paul urged Timothy to teach everyone to pray for government leaders. However, this is no guarantee we will be exempt from this kind of persecution. Like Paul, there are many Christians today who are living in the perfect will of God yet are suffering all kinds of difficulties in this life.

Manipulation and Cruel Theology

One evening, my wife and I were watching an evangelist on television. A mother and father brought their son to the front for prayer and healing. He was in a wheelchair and obviously severely brain-damaged. He could hardly hold up his head and had very little control of other parts of his body.

The evangelist prayed and asked everyone else to pray and believe God, including the parents. But nothing happened. The evangelist prayed again—this time louder—exhorting the audience to believe God. Again, nothing happened.

What happened next made us angry and sad at the same time. The evangelist turned to the parents and audience, accusing everyone of not having enough faith! Imagine the guilt trip this put on this poor, frustrated, and disillusioned couple. What a cruel theology—and what cruel manipulation!

These parents were probably living in God's will and desperately trying to trust God. To blame others for one's own failure is one of the most insensitive things a person can do to other sincere Christians.

"The Earthly Tent We Live In"

Physical and emotional tragedies happen in this world because of the overall effect of sin. But being a Christian and living in God's will does not exempt any of us from the lingering effects of Adam's failure in the Garden of Eden. The whole world was negatively affected and will not be restored until God creates a new heaven and a new earth. Our physical bodies will eventually wear out—sometimes early in life—because of unpredictable and incurable diseases. Some day—but not until then—we will receive our glorified bodies that are imperishable and immortal (1 Cor. 15:50–54).

In the midst of his own suffering, Paul applied this truth to his own life in his second letter to the Corinthians:

> *Now we know that if the earthly tent we live in is destroyed, we have a building from God, an eternal house in heaven, not built by human hands. Meanwhile we groan, longing to be clothed with our heavenly dwelling, because when we are clothed, we will not be found naked. For while we are in this tent, we groan and are burdened, because we do not wish to be unclothed but to be clothed with our heavenly dwelling, so that what is mortal may be swallowed up by life. (2 Cor. 5:1–4)*

Don't misunderstand. If we are Christians and living outside the Lord's will, we will reap what we sow (Gal. 6:7–8). It should not surprise us when we create our own suffering. There are natural consequences to sin, and some sins are so serious people become emotionally and physically ill and have even died (1 Cor. 11:30). However, Paul went on to say that "if we judged ourselves, we would not come under judgment" (11:31).

Principle 2. Life's crises often present the greatest opportunities to demonstrate character and to be a strong witness for Jesus Christ (Phil. 1:12–14).

During Paul's first imprisonment in Rome, he wrote to the Philippians and shared how he was able to flesh out this principle—even when chained to Roman guards:

Now I want you to know, brothers, that what has happened to me has really served to advance the gospel. As a result, it has become clear throughout the whole palace guard and to everyone else that I am in chains for Christ. Because of my chains, most of the brothers in the Lord have been encouraged to speak the word of God more courageously and fearlessly. (Phil. 1:12–14)

Paul attempted to see purpose in his suffering, and he's a great example for all of us. I'm thankful I've never endured the persecution Paul and other Christians have faced down through the centuries—and I hope I never will. However, it's encouraging to know that believers who trust God and see meaning even in their painful experiences draw incredible strength from the Lord Himself. People have been burned at the stake and have faced wild animals with a peaceful countenance. Stephen, of course, is our first example of a Christian who faced death because of his faith. This was an experience Paul never forgot, since he was the one approving this man's martyrdom. Stephen's final breath was a prayer for those who were stoning him. "'Lord,'" he prayed, "'do not hold this sin against them'" (Acts 7:60).

If Stephen faced this kind of death victoriously, how much more should we be able to face our own tragedies which are, in most instances, far less painful and traumatic than Stephen's experience. God desires to use these events in our lives to glorify Himself. This is certainly what Paul was referring to when he wrote to the Romans: "And we know that in all things God works for the good of those who love him, who have been called according to his purpose" (Rom. 8:28).

Personalizing These Principles

The following questions will help you apply these dynamic principles that have been so powerfully illustrated in Paul's life—and in the lives of a multitude of Christians over the centuries:

1. To what extent do you understand that suffering may have nothing to do with specific sins in your life?

   To understand this truth more fully, consider the blind man in John's Gospel, chapter nine. The Pharisees believed his blindness was either caused by the sins of his parents or by his own sins. But Jesus set the record straight when He said, "'Neither this man nor his parents sinned . . . but this happened so that the work of God might be displayed in his life'" (John 9:3).

2. If you are suffering from some physical or emotional malady, in what ways can you see some meaning in your suffering? How can God use this struggle in your own life to be a witness and an encourager to someone else? (see 2 Cor. 1:3–7).

Set a Goal

As you reflect on Paul's example and the principles that he illustrated in his own suffering, ask the Holy Spirit to pinpoint one goal you should set for your own life:

_____

_____

_____

_____

Memorize the Following Scripture

I eagerly expect and hope that I will in no way be ashamed, but will have sufficient courage so that now as always Christ will be exalted in my body, whether by life or by death. For to me, to live is Christ and to die is gain.
PHILIPPIANS 1:20–21

Growing Together

1. Have you ever been confused in your own life about the relationship between suffering and specific sins? How did this confusion affect you?

2. In what ways have you seen Christian leaders blame Christians' problems and their inability to overcome

them on the fact that they don't have enough faith? What
has been the results in their lives?

3. Why is it difficult to see purpose and meaning in suffering?
4. How have you experienced God's strength to endure suffering by seeing some purpose or meaning in what has
   happened?
5. What can we pray for you specifically?

Chapter 12

Finishing the Race with Grace

When my daughter, Robyn, was in college, she ran her first marathon. She trained for months, running six miles during the week and twenty miles on Saturdays. Then came the big day! She finished her twenty-six miles in record time—three hours and thirty-three minutes.

I remember the day well. Her whole family and close friends were cheering her on. But what impacted me the most was our post-race conversation. Five minutes after she crossed the finish line, she was breathing normally and felt and looked great. In spite of her eight-minutes-per-mile achievement for this first marathon, she had "finished the race with grace." Her self-discipline and training had paid off. Needless to say, we were all proud of Robyn.

"Let Us Run with Perseverance" (Heb. 12:1)

Once Paul became a Christian, he had one major goal. No matter what crossed his path—persecution, human tragedies, personal temptations, psychological stress, environmental pressures, or outright satanic opposition—he wanted to finish well. And, of course, he did! He kept his "eyes on Jesus" and won his race with grace (12:2).

When Paul began "his final lap"—which involved several challenging years—he had some very specific plans. Some aspects of these plans he knew for certain were within God's revealed will. Other details involved his own choices, which he always wanted to be in harmony with God's call on his life to preach the gospel to the Gentiles. Some of these details unfolded for Paul. Other plans never materialized.

We've seen both aspects in his life in his letter to the Roman Christians, which he penned on his third missionary journey. "I will go to Spain," he wrote—a trip he planned after he had delivered the gifts of money for the poor in Jerusalem, but on the way he wanted to stop over briefly in Rome (Rom. 15:28). At this point in time, Paul knew by direct revelation from God that he should go to Jerusalem. He also knew he was going to face intense persecution— even imprisonment (Acts 20:23)—but he had no idea that this incarceration would ultimately extend all the way to Rome and his plans to go to Spain would be thwarted. As far as we know, he never made this trip.

Progressive Revelation

What we see in Paul's life is often illustrated in the New Testament. God frequently unveiled and unfolded His will little by little. For example, before Jesus returned to heaven, the apostles asked Him, "'Lord, are you at this time going to restore the kingdom to Israel?'" (Acts 1:6). Jesus responded by telling these men it really was not in God's will for Him to reveal "the times or dates" they were asking about. Rather, they were to return to Jerusalem and wait for the Holy Spirit to come upon them. Then they would become His "witnesses in Jerusalem, and in all Judea and Samaria, and to the ends of the earth" (Acts 1:7–8).

In this instance, Jesus gave His disciples a general outline regarding His will but omitted the specific details that would unfold in years to come. In fact, the Book of Acts unveils many of these details through Luke's historical account. However, nearly two thousand years later God has still not told us everything regarding these times or dates.

Just so, God wanted Paul to know certain things for sure—for example, that he would be persecuted and even imprisoned in Jerusalem—but He withheld details regarding what would happen specifically. And when Paul thought he might be killed, the Lord again appeared and reassured him in the midst of this persecution in Jerusalem that he would indeed be His witness in Rome (23:11). However, the Lord once again did not reveal what that entailed specifically. We, of course, know the outcome because we have the end of the story.

The Voyage to Rome (27:1–28:15)

A Friendly Beginning (27:1–3)

Paul was imprisoned in Caesarea for over two years before he "appealed to Caesar" (24:27; 25:11–12). Festus honored his request and put Paul on board a ship with a number of other prisoners. Both Luke and Aristarchus from Thessalonica accompanied Paul in order to serve him (27:2).

Paul's guard was "a centurion named Julius" who favored him and allowed him a great deal of freedom. In fact, on their very first stop in Sidon, he allowed Paul "to go to his friends so they might provide for his needs" (27:3). Julius no doubt had received a full report from Festus and heard about King Agrippa's conclusion that Paul was innocent and "could have been set free if he had not appealed to Caesar" (26:32).

Contrary Winds (27:4–8)

The trip along the coast of Asia was basically uneventful (see fig. 6). However, when they boarded another ship in Myra that was headed directly for Rome, the scene changed dramatically. The winds were anything but friendly. The going was very slow, tedious, and dangerous, but they finally docked in Fair Havens on the island of Crete.

Paul's Warning (27:9–12)

Paul was sure they were headed for serious trouble. "'Men,'" he warned, "'I can see that our voyage is going to be disastrous and bring great loss to ship and cargo, and to our own lives also'" (27:10). However, when Paul issued this warning, he didn't have a direct word from the Lord since some of the details he shared were inaccurate—and God never makes mistakes. However, Paul knew this route and the climatic conditions very well and he knew from experience that they were headed for trouble. Based on this experience, he believed they would suffer some casualties. However, we know that this specific concern didn't come true, although they did suffer "great loss to ship and cargo."

A Raging Storm and Disaster at Sea (27:13–24)

In spite of Paul's serious warning, the crew didn't take his advice. They decided to sail on to Phoenix, another harbor along the coast of Crete. However, a powerful northeastern

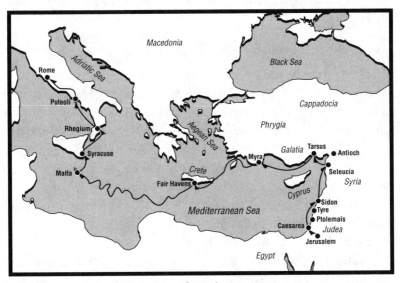

Figure 6
Paul's Journey to Rome

wind drove them out to sea. They had no choice but to lower the anchor and allow the ship to drift with the wind. Luke, who was on board with Paul, relived this frightening experience as he recorded what happened: "When neither sun nor stars appeared for many days and the storm continued raging, we finally gave up all hope of being saved" (27:20).

An Angelic Message (27:21–26)

During this period of hopelessness, Paul received a very direct and specific revelation from God informing him that they would "run aground on some island" and all be saved (27:26). Again, the Lord withheld certain details from Paul, but gave him enough prophetic information so that he could encourage the 276 people on board (27:37).

Since this was a direct revelation from God, the prophecy came true. They hit a sandbar off the island of Malta (see fig. 6). Though the ship was destroyed, everyone made it to safety. Those who could swim jumped overboard and those who couldn't made it to shore on "planks or on pieces of the ship" (27:44).

Miracles on Malta (Acts 28:1–10)

Fortunately, the people on Malta were friendly and caring. But what makes this experience unique are the miracles that God enabled Paul to perform, obviously to demonstrate his apostolic position as well as to provide him with an opportunity to preach the gospel to "listening ears." While helping to build a fire, he survived a deadly snakebite which amazed everyone (28:3–6). Later, he visited Publius, a chief official on the island and healed his father (28:7–8). When word spread about this miraculous event, "the rest of the sick on the island came and were cured" (28:9).

Clearly, the Lord was giving Paul another marvelous opportunity to minister to the Gentiles—including a host of prisoners who survived the shipwreck. Though we are not told how many people opened their hearts to the Lord, we can be certain that many were saved and that a dynamic church was started on this out-of-the-way island.

Safe Arrival (28:11–31)

Three months passed and then everyone boarded another ship that had been wintering at Malta. After stopping in Syracuse and Rhegium, they docked in Puteoli (see fig. 6). At this point, they traveled by land to the city of Rome, a huge metroplex that even in Paul's day numbered at least two million people.

The Roman Imprisonment (28:16–31)

Because of Paul's Roman citizenship, and no doubt because of the recommendation of the centurion, who by this time may have become a Christian, "Paul was allowed to live by himself." Though he had "a soldier to guard him," he had a great deal of freedom (28:16).

Paul wasted no time diving into his ministry. After settling in for three days, he issued an invitation to all of the Jewish leaders in Rome to gather in his home. Paul proceeded to share why he was there. His story created so much interest that these Jewish leaders "arranged to meet Paul on a certain day," and when the word spread, people "came in even larger numbers" (28:23). Watching and listening, Luke recorded that Paul "explained and declared" to these people "the kingdom of God and tried to convince them about Jesus from the Law of Moses and from the Prophets." This went on all day long. Some of the Jews responded positively, but as in other places, there were those who rejected the message of the Messiah (28:24). It was then that Paul once again turned to the Gentiles.

What Paul originally thought would be a stopover in Rome on the way to Spain in order to visit his Christian friends became a two-year opportunity to share the gospel. He "welcomed all who came to see him." Obviously amazed at God's grace, Paul "boldly and without hindrance . . . preached the kingdom of God and taught about the Lord Jesus Christ" (28:30–31).

At this point, Luke ended his historical account, which we call the Book of Acts. But this was not the end of the story. We can learn a great deal about Paul's heart and ministry in Rome from four letters that he wrote from "his own rented house" while chained to a Roman guard. We can also reconstruct some dynamic events from his pastoral epistles—his letters to Timothy and Titus.

The Prison Epistles (Under House Arrest)

Many Bible scholars agree that Paul probably wrote Philippians, Ephesians, Colossians, and Philemon during his two-year stay in Rome—some time during A.D. 61. We are not sure of the sequence. However, no matter what the chronological order, we can gain some unique insights about Paul's perspective during this imprisonment (see chronology chart on p. 6).

The Letter to the Philippians

Paul's letter to the Philippians was prompted by material gifts he had received from the church at Philippi. Hearing that their father in the faith was in prison, they had sent Epaphroditus—perhaps their senior elder and pastor—to deliver these gifts. Paul was overwhelmed by their concern and generosity and he deeply appreciated Epaphroditus's sacrificial service. However, what the Philippians had sent fell short of what Paul needed, and Epaphroditus decided to make up the difference on his own, actually endangering his own life. Though Paul omits specific details, he wrote a letter and penned these grateful words: "Welcome him in the Lord with great joy, and honor men like him, because he almost died for the work of Christ, risking his life to make up for the help you could not give me" (Phil. 2:29–30).

When the Philippians had sent him gifts of money, they had done their best. They may have still been struggling with an impoverished economy. Let's not forget that Paul commended the Macedonian Christians (which certainly included the Philippians) for giving out of their poverty in order to meet the needs of the poor in Jerusalem (2 Cor. 8:1–5). Now once again, they gave sacrificially, this time to help Paul during his Roman imprisonment.

Paul was very encouraged with this act of love. He wanted them to know that he had not forgotten that they were the only church in Macedonia that had helped him financially. After he had left Philippi on his second journey to go to Thessalonica, they had sent "aid again and again when" he "was in need" (Phil. 4:16–17) and now they had assisted him once again.

Paul also reminded them that God would not forget their sacrificial behavior. What they had done would be "credited to" their "account" in heaven. Their gifts, Paul wrote, were "a fragrant offering, an acceptable sacrifice, pleasing to God" (4:18). Furthermore, Paul assured them that the Lord would meet all of their own needs "according to His glorious riches in Christ Jesus" (4:19).

However, when Paul wrote this letter, he did not know whether or not he would ever be set free. God did not reveal this to him. But he was assured that through their prayers for him he would never be hesitant to proclaim the gospel.

We know, however, that after Paul had written to the Philippians, he was pronounced "not guilty" some time near the end of the two-year period mentioned by Luke. In fact, he probably revisited Philippi and thanked them personally for their prayers and gifts.

The Letter to the Ephesians

As Paul spent his days and nights chained to a Roman guard, he often reflected on his missionary experiences.

How could he forget his three fruitful years in Ephesus and his final meeting with the Ephesian elders in Miletus? Predicting at that point that even some of these men would "arise and distort the truth in order to draw away disciples after them" (Acts 20:30), he often wondered what was happening in this church. Knowing that many of them had been converted out of raw paganism and even demonism, he exhorted them to "be strong in the Lord and in his mighty power." He encouraged them to "put on the full armor of God so that" they could take their "stand against the devil's schemes" (Eph. 6:10–11).

Various scholars believe that Paul made this letter generic so it could be circulated to a number of churches that had come into existence in Asia as a result of his daily two-year ministry in the school of Tyrannus. In fact, some of the early manuscripts omit the phrase "to the saints in Ephesus" (Eph. 1:1), which may have been added later by a scribe since Ephesus was the great city where all Asia was touched with the gospel because of Paul's ministry (Acts 19:10). If this was indeed to be a circular letter, it was probably read first in Ephesus and then in the other churches of Asia—which certainly included those mentioned by John in the Book of Revelation (see fig. 5, p. 166).

This is why Paul's prayers in this letter are generic. He prayed for local groups of Christians he had never met before. For example, he wrote, "For this reason, ever since I heard about your faith in the Lord Jesus and your love for all the saints, I have not stopped giving thanks for you, remembering you in my prayers" (Eph. 1:15–16). In other words, Paul had simply received a report about these believers' new life in Christ—which could easily have been the Christians in Smyrna, Pergamum, Thyatira, Sardis, Philadelphia, and Laodicea. In Ephesus, he had not just "heard" about their faith and love—he had experienced it firsthand.

Note also that Paul emphasized unity throughout this letter, underscoring that the Lord "has destroyed the barrier, the dividing wall of hostility" between Jews and Gentiles (2:14).

Christ's "purpose was to create in himself one new man out of the two, thus making peace, and in this one body to reconcile both . . . to God through the cross" (2:15–16).

This is a significant observation since many Jews and Gentiles came to Christ throughout Asia—not just in Ephesus (Acts 19:10). This helps explain why Paul referred to the universal church in this letter (Eph. 1:22; 3:10; 5:23–25, 27, 29, 32) and explained so clearly that there is only one body in Jesus Christ—whether Jews or Gentiles—and we are all "built on the foundation of the apostles and prophets, with Christ Jesus himself as the chief cornerstone" (Eph. 2:20).

The Letter to the Colossians

Colosse was a city in Phrygia. Paul's letter to these Christians is so similar to his letter to the Ephesians that the two are often identified as "twin epistles."

However, Paul had a unique concern for the Colossians. Though he evidently never visited this church, he had heard that they were being exposed to false teaching that reflected both classic Judaism and pagan philosophy. Whatever form it took, this doctrine was undermining their understanding of who Jesus Christ really was. Consequently, Paul warned them:

> *See to it that no one takes you captive through hollow and deceptive philosophy, which depends on human tradition and the basic principles of this world rather than on Christ. For in Christ all the fullness of the Deity lives in bodily form, and you have been given fullness in Christ, who is the head over every power and authority. (Col. 2:8–10)*

Paul also concluded this letter with a prayer request: "Remember my chains" (Col. 4:18; see Eph. 6:19–20). This reference to his incarceration supports the idea that Colossians was not only a letter written approximately at the same time as the letter to the Ephesians, but it was also one of Paul's prison epistles.

The Letter to Philemon

Philemon may have planted the church in Colosse. Perhaps he had heard Paul teach in the lecture hall in Tyrannus on one of his business trips to Ephesus. It's feasible that he responded to the gospel and then carried the good news back to Colosse, led his extended family to Christ (which included his slaves), and then opened his home to others who were interested in the gospel (Philem. 2).

When Philemon became a Christian, his attitude changed dramatically regarding slavery. Taking Paul's instructions seriously, he began to treat his servants as brothers and sisters in Christ (Eph. 6:9; Col. 4:1). Consequently, one of his slaves named Onesimus—who probably had feigned conversion—took advantage of this new freedom and ran away, evidently taking with him some things that didn't belong to him.

In God's providence, Onesimus ended up in Rome and met Paul. He heard the gospel, became a Christian and began to serve Paul (Philem. 10). But, near the end of his imprisonment, Paul decided to send Onesimus back to Philemon to make amends for what he had stolen. Demonstrating both the quality of relationship that Paul had with Philemon as well as his own sense of humor, Paul wrote,

> *So if you consider me a partner, welcome him as you would welcome me. If he has done you any wrong or owes you anything, charge it to me. I, Paul, am writing this with my own hand. I will pay it back—not to mention that you owe me your very self. . . . Confident of your obedience, I write to you, knowing that you will do even more than I ask. (Philem. 17–19, 21)*

We know that Paul was still in prison when he wrote this brief letter since he used the term *prisoner* three times (Philem. 1, 9, 23) and mentioned his *chains* twice more (Philem. 10, 13). It's clear, however, that he expected to be released shortly and hoped to come to Colosse to stay with

Philemon. Consequently, he made a final request: "And one thing more: Prepare a guest room for me, because I hope to be restored to you in answer to your prayers" (Philem. 22).

The Pastoral Epistles

Many scholars believe that after Paul was released from his first imprisonment, he went to Macedonia and Asia, revisiting the churches in these two provinces. He also traveled to Crete with Titus and founded churches in this pagan area. This is based on geographical references in the pastoral Epistles— 1 and 2 Timothy and Titus—that are not mentioned in the Book of Acts.

The First Letter to Timothy

At some point after visiting Asia, Paul wrote his first letter to Timothy after he left him in Ephesus (1 Tim. 1:3). What Paul had predicted would happen when he met with the Ephesian elders in Miletus was happening. Not only were men emerging within the ranks of the elders and teaching false doctrines (1:3–7), but men who were not qualified were also seeking eldership. Consequently, Paul outlined in a classic way the requirements for elders as well as deacons and deaconesses (3:1–13).

Paul dealt with a number of other issues as well, but no concern was more basic in his thoughts than the appointment of qualified leaders. If a church fails at this level, it will disintegrate. However, if there are qualified leaders, most all of the other issues Paul dealt with would be solved.

The Letter to Titus

At some point after Paul was released from prison, he also traveled to the island of Crete and established churches in various locations. A young man named Titus served as his companion. When Paul left the island, he wrote a letter to this fellow missionary, stating that he had left him "in Crete" to "straighten out what was left unfinished." One of his major responsibilities was to "appoint elders in every town" (Titus 1:5).

In many respects, Titus faced the same challenges Timothy faced in Ephesus except that he was helping establish new churches whereas Timothy was dealing with issues in a much older church. Paul outlined the same basic qualifications for eldership in this letter to Titus that he had listed in his first letter to Timothy (compare 1 Tim. 3:1–7 with Titus 1:5–9).

We are not told where Paul was when he wrote this letter to Titus, but we know where he was headed. He planned to send either Artemas or Tychicus to replace Titus and asked him to do his best to join him in Nicopolis, a city located on the west coast of Achaia, about one hundred miles northwest of Corinth (3:12).

Both Paul's first letter to Timothy and his letter to Titus indicate his deep desire to establish Christians in the faith and to make sure local churches were growing and maturing in faith, hope, and love. He knew his time was short and he wanted to do everything possible to conserve his ministry efforts. Thus we see a man who never lost his passion for evangelism but who more and more put his emphasis on the second part of the Great Commission—to establish believers in the faith and to appoint qualified elders in order to reproduce his ministry in and through others (Matt. 28:19–20; Acts 14:21–23; 2 Tim. 2:2).

The Second Letter to Timothy

Paul's second letter to Timothy was also the last epistle he wrote. He was back in prison in Rome. However, this time he was in a dungeon anticipating execution.

According to Tacitus, a reliable Roman historian, a fire broke out in Rome in July, A.D. 64. It spread rapidly and raged for five days. Nero, the Roman emperor, was out of the city at the time but hurried back to deal with the damage. However, it was rumored that he ordered the fire set in order to rebuild the city according to his own selfish interests.

Whatever the circumstances, Nero diverted the rumors from himself and charged Christians with this horrible conflagration. Tacitus' report is bone chilling. He writes:

> Execution was made a matter of sport; some were sewn up in the skins of wild beasts and savaged to death by dogs; others were fastened to crosses as living torches, to serve as lights when daylight failed. Nero made his gardens available for the show and held games in the circus, mingling with the crowd or standing in his chariot in charioteer's uniform.[1]

If Paul were rearrested during this sobering period in Christian history, he would definitely have been charged as a prominent leader of this new sect. Though we are not certain of the facts surrounding his death, Paul knew his time might be short when he wrote his second letter to Timothy. Thus he stated,

> *For I am already being poured out like a drink offering, and the time has come for my departure. I have fought the good fight, I have finished the race, I have kept the faith. Now there is in store for me the crown of righteousness, which the Lord, the righteous Judge, will award to me on that day—and not only to me, but also to all who have longed for his appearing. (2 Tim. 4:6–8)*

If in fact Paul suspected that a martyr's death was just around the corner, he knew "the Lord" would "rescue him"—not from the guillotine—but would escort him "safely to his heavenly kingdom" (4:18).

Paul's Martyrdom

Paul's death is not recorded in Scripture. However, tradition states that he was beheaded outside the city. John Pollock reports:

> They marched Paul to the third milestone on the Ostian Way, to a little pinewood in a glade, probably a place of tombs, known then as Aquae Salviae or Healing Waters, and now as Tre

Fontane where an abbey stands in his honor. He is believed to have been put overnight in a tiny cell, for this was a common place of execution. If Luke was allowed to stay by his window, and if Timothy or Mark had reached Rome in time, the sounds of the night vigil would not be of weeping but singing: "As sorrowful, yet always rejoicing; as dying and, behold, we live."[2]

Paul finished the race with grace. He was ready and anxious to meet the one who died so he might live!

Becoming God's Man Today

Principles to Live By

The biblical principles illustrated by Paul in the final years of his life are foundational, and at the same time they form a divine framework for living for Jesus Christ—from the moment we become Christians until we enter heaven's gates.

Principle 1. God has given all of us certain specifics regarding His perfect will in His revealed Word but gives us a great deal of freedom within these divine guidelines.

It's true that God revealed certain specific information to Paul during his ministry career that is unique simply because he was an apostle. However, even though Paul's calling was much different than ours, the same process is operative in our own lives today. The major difference is that we now have God's revealed will in the New Testament, something that first-century Christians never had. We must remember that the Corinthians may have never read Paul's letter to the Thessalonians and vice versa. The Romans may never have read Paul's letter to the Ephesians and, again, vice versa. We're privileged to have the completed New Testament, twenty-seven books that reveal God's perfect will for our lives. We can be quite certain that thirteen were authored by Paul.

As we read the Bible, it becomes obvious very quickly that God has given us a great deal of freedom in making choices. For example, He doesn't tell us where to live, what college to enroll in, what church to attend, where to work, whom to marry, how many children to have, how much money to make, when to retire, etc. However, in Paul's letters alone, he gives us many very specific statements regarding how to live and how to make proper decisions in all of these situations.

For example, wherever we live or attend college, we are not to participate in sinful activities that violate the will of God. Whatever church we attend, we're to fellowship with true believers and attend regularly. When we choose a business or life mate, we're not to be in relationships with unbelievers that make it difficult, if not impossible, to live fully for the Lord. When it comes to making money, God doesn't tell us "how much is enough," but He tells us always to be generous and to give to God's work regularly and proportionately. In essence, the Bible is filled with divine guidelines to help us make right decisions that are always in harmony with God's will.

Consider, for example, the following selected exhortations taken from each one of Paul's thirteen letters. As you read, note that these letters are listed in the order in which many believe they were written:

Galatians

> *You, my brothers, were called to be free. But do not use your freedom to indulge the sinful nature; rather, serve one another in love. (5:13)*

1 Thessalonians

> *Be joyful always; pray continually; give thanks in all circumstances, for this is God's will for you in Christ Jesus. (5:16–18)*

2 Thessalonians

> *We hear that some among you are idle. They are not busy; they are busybodies. Such people we command and urge in the Lord*

Jesus Christ to settle down and earn the bread they eat. And as for you, brothers, never tire of doing what is right. (3:11–13)

1 Corinthians

I have written you in my letter not to associate with sexually immoral people—not at all meaning the people of this world who are immoral, or the greedy and swindlers, or idolaters. In that case you would have to leave this world. But now I am writing you that you must not associate with anyone who calls himself a brother but is sexually immoral or greedy, an idolater or a slanderer, a drunkard or a swindler. With such a man do not even eat. (5:9–11)

2 Corinthians

Remember this: Whoever sows sparingly will also reap sparingly, and whoever sows generously will also reap generously. Each man should give what he has decided in his heart to give, not reluctantly or under compulsion, for God loves a cheerful giver. (9:6–7)

Romans

Let no debt remain outstanding, except the continuing debt to love one another, for he who loves his fellowman has fulfilled the law. (13:8)

Philippians

Do nothing out of selfish ambition or vain conceit, but in humility consider others better than yourselves. (2:3)

Ephesians

But among you there must not be even a hint of sexual immorality, or of any kind of impurity, or of greed, because these are improper for God's holy people. Nor should there be obscenity, foolish talk or coarse joking, which are out of place, but rather thanksgiving. . . . Therefore do not be partners with them. (5:3–4, 7)

Colossians

Since, then, you have been raised with Christ, set your hearts on things above, where Christ is seated at the right hand of God. Set your minds on things above, not on earthly things. (3:1–2)

Philemon

I pray that you may be active in sharing your faith. . . . (6)

1 Timothy

People who want to get rich fall into temptation and a trap and into many foolish and harmful desires that plunge men into ruin and destruction. For the love of money is a root of all kinds of evil. Some people, eager for money, have wandered from the faith and pierced themselves with many griefs. (6:9–10)

Titus

Teach the older men to be temperate, worthy of respect, self-controlled, and sound in faith, in love and in endurance. Likewise, teach the older women to be reverent in the way they live, not to be slanderers or addicted to much wine, but to teach what is good. Then they can train the younger women to love their husbands and children, to be self-controlled and pure, to be busy at home, to be kind, and to be subject to their husbands, so that no one will malign the word of God. Similarly, encourage the young men to be self-controlled. In everything set them an example by doing what is good. In your teaching show integrity, seriousness and soundness of speech that cannot be condemned, so that those who oppose you may be ashamed because they have nothing bad to say about us. (2:2–8)

2 Timothy

And the things you have heard me say in the presence of many witnesses entrust to reliable men who will also be qualified to teach others. (2:2)

*Principle 2. God promises to give us divine wisdom
when we need it, but we must be careful not to equate
this wisdom on the same level as divine revelation.*

As we have seen, God has given us some very specific instructions and guidelines regarding His perfect will for our lives. At the same time, He gives us a great deal of freedom in making decisions. However, God wants to assist us with these decisions. Consequently, James wrote, "If any of you lacks wisdom, he should ask God, who gives generously to all without finding fault, and it will be given to him" (James 1:5).

With this promise, however, we must remember that what we consider to be "divine insight" may simply be our own selfish desires. Consequently, we must make sure that this "wisdom" we believe is from God is always in harmony with God's specific instructions in the New Testament. If it is not, it is not "divine wisdom."

To avoid making subjective decisions, it's important to consult other mature believers. Though their advice may also reflect their own subjectivity, if they are godly people, they will want God's best for us. Let's remember the Proverb that states, "Where there is no guidance, the people fall, but in abundance of counselors there is victory" (Prov. 11:14, NASB).

Principle 3. God wants all of us to "finish the race with grace."

There is a passage in Hebrews that sounds very much like the apostle Paul. In fact, some Bible scholars believe he actually wrote this letter, which would bring the total number of his epistles to fourteen. Others believe it was authored by Barnabas or perhaps Apollos or some other New Testament leader. However, it really doesn't matter that we know since the epistle to the Hebrews is definitely God's Word. If Paul didn't write it, he would be very pleased with the metaphor used in chapter 12:

Therefore, since we are surrounded by such a great cloud of witnesses, let us throw off everything that hinders and the sin that so easily entangles, and let us run with perseverance the race marked out for us. Let us fix our eyes on Jesus, the author and perfecter of our faith. (Heb. 12:1–2a)

Paul finished the race with grace, and it's God's will that all of us achieve this same goal. With God's help, we can, if we apply the truth inherent in Paul's grand doxology as he concluded his dynamic prayer for the Ephesians:

Now to him who is able to do immeasurably more than all we ask or imagine, according to his power that is at work within us, to him be glory in the church and in Christ Jesus throughout all generations, for ever and ever! Amen. (Eph. 3:20–21)

Personalizing These Principles

As you conclude this study on Paul's life, once again review Paul's statements that have been selected from his thirteen letters (see pp. 215–217). Highlight any exhortations where you want to be more faithful in doing God's will.

Set a Goal

Review what you have highlighted from Paul's exhortations and then ask the Holy Spirit to help you select one goal that you would like to begin to achieve immediately:

_____

_____

_____

_____

Memorize the Following Scripture

Therefore, since we are surrounded by such a great cloud of witnesses,
let us throw off everything that hinders and the sin that so easily entangles,
and let us run with perseverance the race marked out for us.
Let us fix our eyes on Jesus, the author and perfecter of our faith.
HEBREWS 12:1–2a

Growing Together

1. Why is it so important to consult the Word of God in determining the perfect will of God for our lives?

2. What does Paul mean when he refers to being "transformed by the renewing of your mind" (Rom. 12:2) and "to be made new in the attitude of your minds" (Eph. 4:23)? How do these exhortations relate to making decisions that are in the perfect will of God?

3. Would you feel free to share some decisions you've made that have been out of harmony with Scripture and why you would make different decisions if you had it to do over again? Furthermore, since "two wrongs don't make a right," how are you living with the results of a bad decision and at the same time continuing to walk in God's will?

5. What can we pray for you specifically?

Endnotes

Introduction

1. John Strombeck, *Disciplined by Grace* (Grand Rapids: Kregel Publications, 1991).

Chapter 1

1. Robert E. Picirilli, *Paul the Apostle* (Chicago: Moody Press, 1986), 5.
2. F. F. Bruce, *Paul: Apostle of the Heart Set Free* (Grand Rapids: Wm. B. Eerdmans Publishing Co., 1977), 48.
3. Ibid., 46.

Chapter 2

1. Bruce, op. cit., 72. F. F. Bruce references a letter from Lucius, consul of the Romans, that is quoted in 1 Maccabees 15:21.
2. William James, *The Varieties of Religious Experiences* (New York: The Modern Library, 1936), 233–34.

Chapter 3

1. Charles W. Colson, *Born Again* (Old Tappan, New Jersey: Chosen Books, 1976), 57.
2. Some put this gap between 9:20 and 9:21. However, it seems to be more logical to put it between 9:21 and 9:22. The questions raised in 9:21 reflect a very recent experience in the minds of those who lived in Damascus. They understood Paul's reason for coming to their city—to take Christians prisoner. But in verse 22, it appears Paul was not a recent convert to Christianity. He had grown substantially in his knowledge of Christian theology, which correlates with what he describes in his letter to the Galatians, that is, his three years in Arabia.

In other words, I prefer to put this period between Acts 9:21 and 9:22.

3. Well-known scholars disagree as to when Galatians was written and to whom. For example, J. B. Lightfoot in *St. Paul's Epistle to the Galatians,* 10th ed. (London: Macmillan and Co., 1890), 18–35, believes the letter was written after Paul's second missionary journey through northern Galatia. On the other hand, Sir William Ramsay in *An Historical Commentary on St. Paul's Epistle to the Galatians* (New York: G. P. Putnam's Sons, 1900), ii, 478, has contended that "the churches of Galatia" were those of Antioch in Pisidia, Iconium, Derbe, and Lystra, which Paul established on his first missionary journey through southern Galatia. Merrill Tenney in his *New Testament Survey* (Grand Rapids: Eerdmans, 1953), 266–67, points out that "the importance of the difference of interpretation is that the southern Galatian theory allows for an earlier dating of Galatians and for a better explanation of its historical setting." Personally, I agree with Ramsay and Tenney. Hopefully, the way I have arranged the material in this book on Paul helps to confirm the southern Galatian theory.

4. F. F. Bruce, "Legacy of Liberty," *Our Christian History,* Issue 47 (vol. XIV, no. 3).

Chapter 4

1. F. F. Bruce postulates another theory regarding Paul's activities in Arabia and how this may correlate with his reference to the "governor under King Aretas" in the Corinthian letter. He notes: "The 'ethnarch of King Aretas' was probably the representative of the king's subjects who were resident in Damascus, just as the Jewish colony in Alexandria appointed an ethnarch to be their representative and spokesman before the civic and imperial authorities there. But why would the Nabataean ethnarch take this hostile action against Paul, if Paul had spent his time in Arabia in silent contemplation? If, on the other hand, he spent his time there in preaching, he could well have stirred up trouble for himself and attracted the

unfriendly attention of the authorities. Since the Nabataean territory came up almost to the walls of Damascus, the ethnarch, with inadequate body of his fellow-nationals to help him, may have watched the city gate from the outside, so as to arrest Paul if he left the city" (F. F. Bruce, Ibid., 81–82).

2. It's uncertain how long Paul was actually in Jerusalem at this time. We do know he stayed with "Peter" for "fifteen days" (Gal. 1:18). However, if this reference in Galatians correlates with Luke's account in Acts 9:26-30 (which many believe it does), Paul was there long enough to "move about freely in Jerusalem, speaking boldly in the name of the Lord" (Acts 9:28). This implies a longer period than just fifteen days.

Chapter 5

1. John B. Polhill, *The New American Commentary: Acts* (Nashville: Broadman & Holman, 1992), 174.

2. John Pollock, *The Man Who Shook the World* (Wheaton: Victor Books, 1972), 36.

Chapter 7

1. F. F. Bruce, *Paul: Apostle of the Heart Set Free*, 134.

2. Some believe that this first missionary journey probably took place during the years A.D. 46 to 48. Admittedly, this is only an estimate based on the dating of earlier and later events. See *The Zondervan Pictorial Encyclopedia of the Bible*, vol. 4, edited by Merrill C. Tenney (Grand Rapids: Zondervan Publishing House, 1975, 1976), 636.

Chapter 8

1. It's certainly proper to ask how we can be certain of this sequence of events. Obviously, we can't be sure. However, it's a logical conclusion based on what happened. Luke allowed for this sequence when he recorded that Paul and Barnabas "stayed there [in Antioch] a long time with the disciples" (Acts 14:28).

Chapter 9

1. Note the singular pronouns: "he went through Syria and Cilicia" (15:41); "he came to Derbe and then to Lystra" (16:1).

2. When you read about Paul's weaknesses that are reflected in his letter to the Galatians, you might ask how this letter could be the divinely inspired Word of God yet include this kind of humanness. I can only respond by saying that God can weave this kind of frailty into His inspired revelation without violating the authoritative message to believers of all time. This is the miracle of divine inspiration.

Chapter 10

1. Many Christians ignore the context in Acts, chapters 1 and 2, when they interpret these events on the day of Pentecost. Luke clearly reported that it was the apostles (the "eleven" plus Matthias) who experienced this special filling of the Spirit (see 1:26; 2:1) which was accompanied by "tongues of fire that separated and came to rest on each of them" as well as being able to "speak in other tongues" or languages (2:3–4). All the pronouns that follow Luke's reference to the apostles refer to these twelve men. Furthermore, the people who heard them speaking various languages were totally surprised since they identified them as "Galileans" (2:7). This is significant since all of the apostles were indeed from Galilee. Later, Peter referred to "the eleven" as those who had just had this unique experience (2:14–15).

2. See the references to both Jew and Gentile converts in the following verses: 19:10, 17–20; 20:21.

3. This is obviously a generalization. Luke did not mean to imply that every single person in the whole area heard the gospel. It does imply that multitudes were exposed to the truth since many people responded to Paul's message.

4. Luke recorded that the value of these books was fifty thousand drachmas. A drachma was equal to a day's wages.

Assuming that the average American makes one hundred dollars per day, this would total five million dollars.

5. Many scholars agree that Paul wrote this letter not only to the church in Ephesus but designed it to be a circular letter to be read in the churches throughout Asia. If so, this is why Paul frequently used the word *church* in this letter to refer to the universal body of Christ (Eph. 1:22; 3:10, 21; 5:23–25, 27, 29, 32).

6. J. H. Hadfield, *Childhood and Adolescence* (Baltimore: Penguin, 1962), 134.

7. For a detailed study of each of these qualities, see Gene A. Getz, *The Measure of a Man* (Ventura, California: Regal, 1995).

Chapter 11

1. The believers in Achaia and Macedonia were not the only Christians who participated in contributing to this relief fund. It also included the churches in Galatia and certainly in Asia. Gaius and Timothy both lived in Galatia and Trophimus was from Ephesus (Acts 21:29). In fact, Paul made it clear in his first letter to the Corinthians that when he left Antioch on his third journey and traveled through the "region of Galatia and Phrygia," he made this need known (compare 1 Cor. 16:1–4 with Acts 18:23). These observations indicated that Paul had planned his trip to Jerusalem right at the beginning of his third missionary journey.

Chapter 12

1. Tacitus, *Annals* XV. 44. 3-8, as quoted by F. F. Bruce, *Paul: Apostle of the Heart Set Free* (Grand Rapids: Wm. B. Eerdman's Publishing Company, 1977), 442.

2. John Pollock, op. cit., 308.

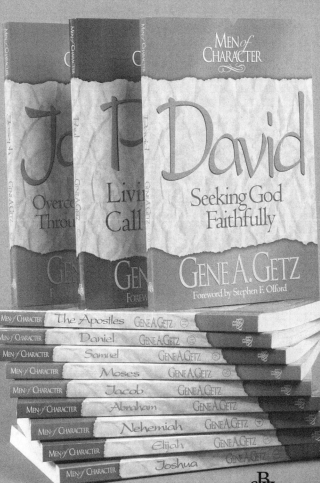